THE DIY GUIDE
··· *to* ···

BUILDING
A Family
THAT LASTS

THE DIY GUIDE to BUILDING A Family THAT LASTS

12 TOOLS FOR IMPROVING YOUR HOME LIFE

GARY CHAPMAN
and SHANNON WARDEN

NORTHFIELD PUBLISHING

CHICAGO

Edited by Elizabeth Cody Newenhuyse
Interior design: Erik M. Peterson
Cover design: Faceout Studios
Cover photo of table and chairs copyright © 2019 by Westend61/Gettyimages (647331513).
Cover photo of pens copyright © 2019 by Adha Ghazali/Shutterstock (1019514556).
Cover photo of notebook copyright © 2018 by Martí Sans/Stocksy (1914607).
All rights reserved for all of the above photos.
Gary Chapman photo: P.S. Photography
Shannon Warden photo: Gina Childress, Picture This Photography

Library of Congress Cataloging-in-Publication Data

Names: Chapman, Gary D., 1938- author.
Title: The DIY guide to building a family that lasts : 12 tools for improving your home life / Gary Chapman and Shannon Warden.
Other titles: Do it yourself guide to building a family that lasts
Description: Chicago : Northfield Publishing, 2019. | Includes bibliographical references.
Identifiers: LCCN 2019009731 (print) | LCCN 2019017266 (ebook) | ISBN 9780802497840 () | ISBN 9780802419149
Subjects: LCSH: Families--Religious aspects--Christianity. | Families--Religious life.
Classification: LCC BT707.7 (ebook) | LCC BT707.7 .C47 2019 (print) | DDC 248.4--dc23
LC record available at https://lccn.loc.gov/2019009731

ISBN: 978-0-8024-1914-9

We hope you enjoy this book from Northfield Publishing. Our goal is to provide high-quality, thought-provoking books and products that connect truth to your real needs and challenges. For more information on other books and products that will help you with all your important relationships, go to www.moodypublishers .com or write to:

Northfield Publishing
820 North LaSalle Boulevard
Chicago, IL 60610

1 3 5 7 9 10 8 6 4 2

Printed in the United States of America

FROM GARY:

Dedicated to my wife, Karolyn,
daughter, Shelley, and son, Derek,
with whom I have experienced numerous
home renovations!

FROM SHANNON:

To Mama and Daddy (Kenny and Sandra Prater),
thank you for loving and lasting and
showing me how to do the same.
To Stephen, Avery, Carson, and Presley,
you are my dream team!
I love being "all-in" with you.

CONTENTS

INTRODUCTION

EVER WATCH A HOME IMPROVEMENT show on television? Or maybe you've done your own home improvement projects. It is truly amazing to see the big reveal—that moment when dreams and hard work result in a beautiful new space or completely renovated home. What used to be old and out-of-style is now transformed and fresh! We ask ourselves, "Why did we wait so long to do this?"

My coauthor, Shannon, and I enjoy home improvement shows and projects. However, we specialize in a different kind of home improvement. We're marriage and family counselors who have the great privilege of sitting with individuals and couples who are dreaming of a new home life. They don't want a new family; they just need new tools to improve the family life they've got. More specifically, they want to communicate more effectively and love their family members better. They want to figure out how to encourage their children, create more peace in their home, and establish and maintain more effective boundaries.

Do you see the similarities in the home improvement we talk about in our counseling office and the literal home improvement? In both cases, frustration or boredom with the old leads to increased desire for change. Desire leads to plans. Plans lead to action steps. And action steps lead to a beautifully transformed home . . . or home life.

Literal home improvement and home life improvement do, of course, have their differences. One difference is that people can pay contractors to renovate for them as opposed to them having to do renovations on their own. Improving our relationships doesn't quite work like that. As counselors, Shannon and I don't go into a home and create an all-new home life for the people with whom we work. Instead, we help people learn to DIY—do it yourself.

In our counseling role we listen, help people clarify their relationship goals, and collaborate with them to make plans and take steps to accomplish those goals. We also teach and help people develop new insights and relationship skills, or "tools" they need to improve their home life. It is our clients who then have to decide how motivated they are to tackle the changes they need to make at home to accomplish the new home life they desire.

That's the hard part, isn't it—the follow-through! Think about it. If you and your spouse have some negative communication patterns that have built up over several years, reversing those patterns doesn't happen overnight. Both of you have to commit to make the change, make daily effort toward the goal, and little by little positively reinforce and sustain the good changes that you're making together as a team. Sounds easy, but it's not, because we all run out of steam over time. We get lazy, take our relationships for granted, and assume that they'll hold up indefinitely despite not only our lack of significant improvements but also our lack of basic relationship maintenance.

We don't just struggle in our marriage relationships; we also struggle to be the good parents we desire to be. Shannon and I regularly work with parents who say things like, "I need to spend more time with my children, but I'm just so busy with work," and "I don't want my child to be the only one who doesn't have the technology the other kids have." These parents, like many others, are trying to create better work-life balance and healthier boundaries. They're not trying necessarily to be "perfect" parents; they merely recognize and want to change some ongoing issues at home before it's too late and their children are grown and gone from home.

> We get lazy, take our relationships for granted, and assume that they'll hold up indefinitely.

You likely can relate to these examples and recognize areas for improvement in your family that have needed attention for a long time. You may have even tried over time to make those changes, but just haven't had the success you hoped for. But you haven't given up! Instead, you've committed to investing in your family and home life. That's why you're reading *The DYI Guide to Building a Family That Lasts*. You're curious—is it really possible for me to have the home life I want with the people I love? The answer is yes! You're not as far away as you think from having the transformed home life you long for. You already have the desire for improved relationships at home. You're willing to put in the sweat equity (hard work). You just need new tools. That's where Shannon and I come in. We've filled this book with encouraging, practical insights and how-tos to serve as the new tools you'll need to accomplish your home improvement goals.

Along with sharing successful relationship tools, we use literal home improvement examples throughout the book to help drive home our points. We talk about everything from everyday household cleanup to major renovations, not because we're home improvement contractors, but because we're home improvement counselors. Our hope is that you'll both learn from and enjoy the home improvement metaphor as you read and work on your home improvement project.

So grab your toolbox! Let's get to work!

HOME IMPROVEMENT GOAL:

Demolish selfishness.

HOME IMPROVEMENT TOOL:

Build kindness.

Chapter 1

BUILDING
KINDNESS

Share the load ... the laundry load, that is!

#yougottalaugh

GARY: Early on, I wasn't considerate enough of Karolyn's needs. Thankfully, she was (and is) persistent in letting me know. #Consider me way more considerate now than when we started out!

SHANNON: My kids won't let me not consider their needs. They're sweet, but very verbal . . . and very assertive. #Consider me out for the count at bedtime!

"THAT'S MINE!" "You're in my space." "We don't ever do what I want to do."

Do you frequently hear comments like these around your home? Are they typically said with an angry or critical attitude?

If you answered yes to these questions, you're not alone!

Comments and attitudes such as these suggest that your family, like many others, deals with selfishness. You're also not alone if "less selfishness" is at the top of your home improvement list.

For starters, you may be tired of your children arguing over toys or fighting about who gets to sit by the window or eat the last cookie. Like most parents, you just want a little peace and quiet. You ask, "Why can't you kids just get along?"

Plus, you may desire that your children grow up knowing how to share and get along with others. You realize that now, not later, is the time to train them in these skills.

Then there's you and your spouse. You each may wish the other person would step up their share of the work around the house or just be more supportive of your ideas and feelings. Cleaning, laundry, and bills are not going to do themselves, after all! You ask, "I thought we were a team. Why aren't you helping me?"

Just sharing a house can spark problems. If your family shares bathrooms, you know what I mean . . .

You have to wait to get in the bathroom and sometimes have to deal with sharing the space with another family member. Then you've got the issue of little to no counter space, which means other people's stuff gets mixed in with your stuff. For family members who prefer clean spaces, this can also mean a messy kid—or spouse—may regularly be undoing your tidying-up efforts. Or how about the person who takes forever in the shower?

Waiting. Sharing. Protecting our space and our stuff. Not fun! If we were talking about literal home improvement, a bathroom renovation in this case would definitely be much appreciated. I can imagine renovators removing a wall, repositioning the shower or toilet, or updating the bathroom vanity to modernize and maximize space.

Similarly, selfishness in the family makes us feel cramped for space and time. We can't touch each other's stuff without backlash. We may be criticized if we want or take time to ourselves. Or we may fail to understand or offer help to each other when that help could go a long way in easing another's stress. Although the physical space issues that necessitate sharing can be annoying, the selfish attitudes behind the backlash, criticism, or lack of understanding can be even more frustrating.

Of course, we expect selfishness from small children. In fact, it doesn't seem to take them long to realize that they don't like someone messing with their stuff. But many adults continue well beyond childhood holding on to selfishness in one area or another. Our loved ones may call us out for our selfishness. We, too, may know we're being selfish. But it's up to us to decide whether or not we will resist our selfish tendencies for the good of our home life.

We hear about this all the time as we counsel families. Nearly everyone would like to build a family less selfish, more kind and considerate. But before we try to fix the problem, we validate people's feelings because that's an important part of home improvement—simply acknowledging that family members' thoughts and feelings matter. We then spend time talking through personal expectations and defining what selfishness is and how it negatively impacts family relations.

As part of those home improvement talks, I work with people to see that not all "selfish" thoughts and feelings are bad. Thoughts and feelings can sometimes represent valid desires for consideration or help. After all, a child may not truly be selfish in the worst sense of the word; she is merely young and heartbroken over having to share a favorite toy. Or a husband may have worked diligently to get household chores done in time to watch his favorite team play on television; he isn't necessarily being selfish because of making a little time for his own special interests.

Not all "selfish" thoughts and feelings are bad.

While increasing understanding is an important improvement tool, in this chapter, the primary tool I want to encourage you to add to your home improvement toolbox is kindness, and more specifically, consideration of your family's needs.

Why kindness?

You've been kind throughout your life, so you know what kindness is. It's making sure your spouse has his or her favorite peanut butter as opposed to buying the cheaper brand you'd prefer to buy; it's listening to your spouse or child vent when you'd prefer to be reading your magazine or taking a nap; and it's giving up watching your favorite home improvement television show so that you can spend time with your child who wants to watch SpongeBob.

You've also benefited from the kindness of others. So you know how it feels when your spouse texts you to check in on how you're doing, when your child picks up her toys to surprise you when you come home from work, and when your family treats you special on your birthday.

Why are you kind? Why did someone else's consideration of you matter? I believe the answer is the same for both questions—consideration makes people feel like their needs matter. We want our loved ones to know their needs matter to us, and we want to know that our needs matter to them. Selfishness, on the other hand, conveys the opposite—that our needs are more important than their needs. Just as no physical home is perfect, no home life is perfect. We're human, so we know to expect some selfishness. But the less selfishness and the more kindness, the better!

 ## DRAWING UP THE PLANS

When renovating our home, we, or a contractor, envision in our minds, then draw on paper or computer what our desired improvements will look like. I encourage families to do the same thing with their home life improvement plans, or "blueprints." You already know what you don't want. But what *do* you want?

How will you and your family be more considerate of one another going forward? What would home life look like if you and they were more considerate of one another? I encourage you to think through your specific goals and talk with your family about it as well. They may be curious about and encouraged by your desire to involve them in a home improvement project. They also may have helpful insights and input about how to decrease selfishness and increase consideration. You're wise to hold these types of family meetings during dinner, at bedtime, or at other peaceful times when you have your family's attention. This is generally more effective than trying to discuss and decide upon family goals during times of conflict.

You might begin by asking each family member to make a list of the complaints they have heard from others. Perhaps Mom has complained that Brent does not put his toys in the closet when he has finished playing. The complaint reveals an area where Brent can be more considerate.

To help you generate ideas for increasing consideration, let me share with you a few examples of people with whom I or Shannon have worked over time.

One mom told Shannon, "I feel like my kids fight all of the time. I guess they're no more selfish than the average teenagers, but I wish they could talk through problems and get along better."

> We should work for less conflict rather than no conflict.

Shannon reminded the mom that getting along, or having less conflict, is a well-intentioned goal. Some parents unrealistically want no conflict at all. Instead, we should work for less conflict rather than no conflict. We will share practical help in resolving conflicts in chapter 4.

Another mom shared with me that she was tired of fussing at her children to help around the house. Her home improvement plans included wanting the children to follow through with their chores as expected rather than she or her husband having to remind them. For this to happen, we need to communicate clear consequences of what happens when they don't do their chores. Make a list of chores for each child and the consequences if they do not complete the chores on time. Then consistently apply the consequences. Affirm the children when they do the chores in a timely manner.

Here is an idea that many couples have found helpful. Agree to share with each other one request each week as to what would make life easier for you. Before you make the request, tell your spouse two things you like or appreciate about them. Then make your request. Notice I say "request" and not "demand"! You are giving them information. It is their choice to consider your request or not. Once the two of you begin to make changes to please the other, your family life will be enhanced.

DO-IT-YOURSELF

You're perhaps familiar with the phrase "do-it-yourself," which is commonly abbreviated DIY. When it comes to home renovations, DIY means that instead of calling a professional, you complete a home improvement project on your own.

For Shannon and me, DIY takes on a whole new meaning. Yes, families must do their own work; Shannon and I can't go house to house fixing people's families. But more than doing your own work, DIY for us means that you have to model for your family the behavior you want to see them exhibit. You must do it yourself. In this case, if you want more consideration in your children and spouse, you must increase your consideration of your children and your spouse.

Here is where it gets tough for many of us. We would rather talk about how selfish and inconsiderate our spouse or children are than look at our own selfishness and lack of consideration. That's a bad habit that we have to break if we want to make real and lasting home life improvements.

> You have to model for your family the behavior you want to see them exhibit.

A good DIY starting place in the area of kindness is to step up your self-awareness. Watch how you interact with your loved ones. Notice when you're being inconsiderate and the effects it has on your family. Or better yet, notice when your family is upset with you, then ask yourself, how am I being inconsiderate of my family at this moment? Also notice your reaction to what you perceive as selfishness by your loved ones. Are you reacting to their selfishness with your own selfishness? On the flip side of that, did your selfishness and lack of consideration of their needs in some way contribute to their selfish behavior?

The fact that you haven't closed the book at this point is a good sign that you're willing to consider DIY. It's hard to look at our own shortcomings, but we clearly see shortcomings of others. Through a more compassionate lens, we can increase our self-awareness and take more responsibility for our own selfishness.

ALL-IN BUDGET

My favorite home improvement shows often talk to people about their "all-in budget." A couple will say, for example, that they have $100,000 for home renovations. The renovation team then works within the couple's budget to provide as many of the desired renovations as possible within that budgeted amount.

For Shannon and me, "all-in" in home life improvement means two things. First, families need to be all *in*, or fully committed to making change, even though it may take lots of hard work. Second, families need to be *all* in so that no one family member is expected to take on the brunt of the work. You are a team, after all, and need to work together to improve your relationships and interactions with one another.

Commitment needs to be initiated and sustained by the parents. Just as home renovators often work with construction crews, you as parents are the crew chiefs and must lead well and involve your family (your crew) so that more progress can be accomplished more quickly. If you lack commitment as the team leader, your family will also likely lack commitment.

Your unity is an important foundation that positively affects all other family relationships. As the old saying goes, "many hands make light work." Home life improvements are family projects! You can't "make" people change, and you can't do each other's part to bring about the change you desire. But if as a couple you are working together, and you lead your family to join you, the possibilities for change are limitless!

Commitment and teamwork are important home life improvement tools that help make change more achievable. How can commitment and teamwork foster consideration of others? Think about your own plans for demolishing selfishness at home.

If your plan includes family members talking through problems rather than arguing for their own way, then commitment and teamwork to increase consideration might mean that you and your family call a "time out" before or during an argument to cool down and approach the matter more calmly. You can then hear better what the other person's point of view is and perhaps share your perspective in a more reasonable way so that the other person can better understand your viewpoint.

Or perhaps one of your family goals is that people consider the importance of each other's personal space. You and your family talk about why Mom's home office is special to her, why Dad's workshop is special to him, why a brother's collection is special to him, why a sister's art table is important to her. Each of you commits to honoring these special spaces in reasonable ways, and then you remember to thank each other whenever another person honors their commitment. Commitment and teamwork are needed to make your personal space goal possible.

Right about now you might be saying, "Gary, that will never work in our house. We've tried!" You're right, it won't work unless you have a plan, unless you DIY, and unless you and your family are all in!

Jeremy and Lori had similar doubts. After several halfhearted attempts at change, they decided it was time to step up their efforts. They explained to their children what kindness is and what they wanted it to look like for them as a family. Lori told me later, "The children really got into it and started calling everybody out, including us, whenever we were inconsiderate toward someone. At first, that was a little annoying, but it actually started to sink in. We're still not perfect, but we've come a long way."

SWEAT EQUITY

Time and effort! As in literal home improvement, we just can't seem to get away from work, can we? Although we wish we could automatically have the home life and relationships we want with no extra effort on our part, that's just not realistic for any individual, couple, or family. We have to put in the hard work, or sweat equity, to have the home life we desire.

In chapter 1, we've explored the home improvement tool of consideration. The following is a recap of important tips for decreasing selfishness and building kindness in our home:

- **Be realistic.** Children don't come fully equipped with consideration skills. As you establish your home improvement goals, factor in your kids' age and stage of life so that you're not asking more of them than they're developmentally ready to accomplish. In fact, simple, achievable goals will help foster the kindness you desire.
- **Be patient.** Adults don't break selfish habits overnight.

You all need time to learn new habits. However, this shouldn't be an open-ended excuse for not considering and attending to the needs of your loved ones.

- **Don't stop believing!** We sometimes see home improvement shows and think, "That's out of my range." We may also look at other families in the same way: "I wish we could be like them, but we never will." Many families are discouraged and doubt their potential for change. But this is where you have to decide: "Do I do nothing? Or do I do *something*?" Doing something—even making the smallest effort—is progress. As Shannon often says, "Small steps forward are better than big steps backward."

- **Prioritize.** Because small steps take time, you're wise to prioritize which attitudes and behaviors you want to target for home improvement. I like to call these "work orders," or the specific tasks families work on at any one time that help them accomplish their home improvement goals. In building kindness, you may want to focus on some simple but powerful work orders such as: 1) we notice and say thank you to each other every chance we get; 2) we offer a genuine apology anytime a loved one calls us on our selfishness; and 3) we ask each other how we can help one another.

- **Expect setbacks.** Inevitably in literal home improvement, there are unexpected issues that arise and require extra money, time, and effort to correct. Similarly, when families begin working on their home life and relationships, there will be setbacks of one kind or another. My encouragement to you is to acknowledge when a setback is happening. For example, perhaps you and your spouse have enjoyed several instances of mutual consideration, but then get into a major argument about something altogether different. This can be a setback to the home improvement work you're doing. But commit to yourself and to each other that you won't let that setback deter you from your home improvement projects.

- **Work together.** They say, "Teamwork makes the dream work." That's true in literal home improvement and in our efforts to improve our home life. Believing in and committing to teamwork is, itself, a considerate mindset. A strong team is made up of strong teammates who value their teammates as much as they value themselves. Team-minded families unite and work together to avoid the division that selfishness can cause.

BIG REVEAL

Imagine this. Your family loads into the car, and you hear your six-year-old say to his younger sister, "I don't mind. You can sit there." Or you know your wife is equally exhausted after a long day at work, yet she says, "Sure, I'll take the trash out." And you begin to hear and see these attitudes and behaviors more often than in the past. You think, "Kindness! It's working!"

I don't know what your "big reveal" moments will look like, but they will multiply over time as you and your loved ones get more serious about working through challenges and working toward new and improved ways of being with each other.

Home improvement shows often end with their own kind of big reveal. A couple has waited anxiously and now gets the first glimpse and the first walk-through of their newly improved home. They sometimes say things like, "I don't even recognize it. That's the same house, right?"

I encourage you to celebrate with your family as you and they begin considering each other in little and big ways. Notice kindness, celebrate kindness, and enjoy the fruit of your labor, which, in this case, will be less selfishness and more consideration.

TALK IT OVER

1. What are some examples of selfishness you've witnessed in your home in recent days? What did you do about it?

2. What challenges hamper your efforts at decreasing selfishness?

3. What makes it hard for us to regard one another as more important than ourselves?

4. What is one way you can DIY and model more kindness toward your loved ones this next week?

5. What is one teamwork goal you and your family can begin working toward to show greater consideration of each other this next week?

· · · · · · · · · · ·

HOME IMPROVEMENT GOAL:
Decrease disrespect.

HOME IMPROVEMENT TOOL:
Increase gratitude.

· · · · · · · · · · ·

Chapter 2

INCREASING GRATITUDE

Floors are made to be walked all over; loved ones are not.

#yougottalaugh

GARY: Our daughter was pretty easy to raise, but our son . . . well, let's just say he was really talented at testing our patience.
#Grateful for our kids, then and now!

SHANNON: I don't mind killing a bug or spider, but if Stephen is around, he springs into action and does that job for me.
#Grateful for my spider man!

"I WORK MY TAIL OFF, and she never acts like she cares."

"Everybody expects Mom to do everything. But nobody ever expresses appreciation, let alone lift a finger."

"My daughter doesn't call me; she just texts. And usually, that's only when she needs money."

"Our son is happy to eat us out of house and home, but helping us clean that house and home, forget about it!"

Over the years, I've heard many versions of these statements. Many wives and husbands feel unappreciated—by both their spouses and their kids.

But lack of appreciation is just one of many forms of disrespect. Other disrespectful attitudes and behaviors include dismissing each other's personal goals as insignificant or silly, putting each other down verbally either privately or publicly, and knowingly going against each other's wishes or undermining each other's objectives.

These various forms of disrespect are sometimes infrequent and subtle, so much so that you or your loved ones might simply show grace to one another and just let it slide. For example, your child may say something like, "You're the worst parent ever" when you revoke his electronics privileges. Or your spouse may thoughtlessly track muddy shoes into the kitchen after you've recently mopped the floor. You know your child is mad, and you know your spouse is in a hurry, so you carry on without arguing further with your child and without criticizing your spouse for the spot mop you'll be doing.

Other times, disrespect taps into something deep inside us. We can't let it slide and are compelled to respond because we feel that we've been discredited or taken advantage of. For example, perhaps your child regularly and unapologetically tells you how terrible a parent you are. Or maybe your spouse routinely messes up the house but rarely helps clean it. In instances such as these, our response might range from a gentle request for respect to a furious verbal assault.

How we choose to respond to patterns of disrespect either enhances or chips away at our relationships. We cannot ignore such disrespect. To do so will lead to resentment. On the other hand, responding harshly is not helpful and can actually make things worse. An ancient Hebrew proverb says, "A gentle answer turns away wrath, but a harsh word stirs up anger."[1] And so, we strive for an assertive but gentle response to disrespect.

Shannon shares this from her own marriage. "I spent a lot of time earlier in our marriage being quietly angry at Stephen for what I perceived to be his desire to save every dollar. I knew we had different mindsets about saving and spending, but I didn't appreciate what came across to me as 'controlling the money.'"

Stephen also had his own disrespect issues toward Shannon. Once when they were talking with a contractor about her dreams of developing their six-acre property and buying two small adjacent lots, Stephen made fun of her plans. He sarcastically said to the contractor, "Yeah, she's going to buy all the land around before it's done with."

"I told him he didn't have to share my dream, but I didn't appreciate him putting my dreams down."

"I sat on my feelings for a while rather than lashing out. Then, the next day, I told him that he didn't have to share my same dream, but I didn't appreciate him putting my dreams down. He sincerely apologized, and I was willing to forgive."

Shannon and Stephen's relationship has grown stronger as a result of their ongoing efforts to understand, trust, and appreciate one another. They've also helped their relationship by taking personal responsibility for their own disrespectful attitudes and behaviors. A willingness to apologize is another good relationship tool that makes it easier to appreciate and support one another in our home improvement efforts.

How we choose to view and respond to disrespect in our home life makes me think about how we treat the floors in our homes. Of course, in the case of floors, we have no choice but to "walk all over" them. But after a while, the wear and tear adds up. Because floors are so visible and serve such an important purpose in our houses, we have to take steps to improve them.

In the literal world of home improvement, we have many options for improving our floors. I already mentioned the spouse who tracked mud across the floor. That's a simple fix—we just mop the floor (again). Other common floor-related home improvement projects include ripping up and replacing old carpet with new carpet, installing new or refinishing old hardwood floors, and laying decorative tile floors. These improvements usually look and feel amazing, and we proudly show them off to our guests.

WHY GRATITUDE?

See the comparison? Walking all over our loved ones, or disrespecting them, is not ideal; the wear and tear over time can do great damage in our relationships. To protect and improve these relationships, we need to care for and appreciate our loved ones like we care for and appreciate new floors. With this in mind, I invite you to add the home improvement tool of gratitude to your toolbox.

Why gratitude?

Research has consistently shown that gratitude contributes to better mental and physical health, increased enjoyment of life, and stronger relationships. That's fairly convincing evidence in favor of gratitude.

You already know the positive potential for gratitude if you had the good fortune of growing up in an encouraging, supportive family. Your family was grateful for you, and you, in turn, were grateful for them. Because of that foundation, now as a married person and/or parent, you likely naturally want to convey and encourage a similar gratitude in your own home life.

If you didn't grow up in a family that valued you, you likely longed then and may still long now to be cared for and appreciated. You missed out on an important foundation for positive relationships, but you desire home improvement, so you hope and work to create positive relationships with your spouse and children. Gratitude is a hallmark of positive relationships.

Gratitude is something that psychologist Dr. Carl Rogers

understood. He taught about the concept of unconditional, positive regard, which means that no matter what, we as human beings have value. In addition to promoting this viewpoint, Rogers's approach to counseling emphasizes that we each have innate strengths that make us capable of working through life's challenges. I encourage families to see their loved ones in this light because it helps us to better trust that our loved one's approach to life is valid and purposeful. When we see each other as valuable, we are less likely to show disrespect in our words and actions.

> Family is the most important place for people to feel that they belong.

Another helpful counseling concept is that of *belonging*. People want to feel like they genuinely belong and have value within their families and communities. Family is the most important place for people to feel that they belong. When we criticize or disrespect a family member, we are hurting one of our own.

You may be saying about now, "Gary, you're out of touch with reality. Families disagree and argue. We don't always see eye to eye." Right! We will never have the same thoughts, feelings, or perspectives. We have different personality types, approaches to life, and communication styles. But as much as we know this to be true, families can learn to respect their differences. Instead, we often battle with each other to "win" arguments or to change another person's point of view. In the process of fighting for our rights and viewpoints, we end up disrespecting the rights and viewpoints of others. That's where gratitude comes into play. The more gratitude or appreciation we feel for each other, the less disrespect we're likely to experience.

 # DRAWING UP THE PLANS

First, let's identify how disrespect is hurting your family. Let me suggest that you ask each member to make a list of how they feel when another family member shows disrespect for them. Then bring them together and let each person read their list to the whole family. This is not a time to get defensive, but a time to receive information. Now you can see how disrespect is hurting family relationships.

The next step is for each family member to say to the person who felt disrespected, "I am sorry I hurt you. I hope you will forgive me. I am going to work on changing that."

Now, let me ask a personal question. What is your plan for working on replacing disrespect with gratitude? May I offer a suggestion? Give each family member several sheets of paper. Ask them to write the name of a family member at the top of each page. These are going to be your gratitude sheets. This week the assignment is to list three things that you appreciate about that person. For example: I appreciate that Mom fixes breakfast for us. I appreciate that Dad plays ball with me. Announce that next week in your family time you will read these to each other.

The next week you will add two more "gratitudes" to

each name, and report these to the family. Do the same for six weeks, and you will begin to see the emotional climate in your family enhanced. It is difficult to be harsh, critical, and condemning when you learn to express gratitude.

Perhaps increased gratitude might lead to more unity between you and your spouse when it comes to parenting styles. So many parents disrespect each other unintentionally and intentionally when they undermine each other's parenting.

When faced with big parenting decisions, the couple might agree to not discuss the situation in front of the children. They may, instead, in a show of gratitude for one another, call a parents' business meeting to calmly discuss and come to agreement about the situation. This togetherness is a sign to each other and to the children that Mom and Dad value each other and are united.

The couple would then return to the children with their decision and, thereafter, back each other up when it comes to following through with that decision.

Some parents treat their children in very unkind and condescending ways. The parents then later wonder why their children are disrespectful and lack gratitude. If we as adults are disrespectful in our attitudes and behavior toward our children, we convey critical, dismissive, and belittling messages that suggest to them, "You don't belong here." Respectful treatment of our children, even when we're upset with them, helps us more clearly convey a loving message of "you do belong here. I love you, but you know you broke the rule. So let's talk about what happened and what the consequences are."

In whatever ways your family is struggling with disrespect, and whatever your vision for increasing grateful attitudes and behaviors, be grateful for the family you have and hopeful for the family you and they may still yet become.

 # DO-IT-YOURSELF

As we noted in chapter 1, we're sometimes better blamers of others than we are blamers of ourselves. We see, hear, and feel our spouse's and children's disrespect of us, but we don't so readily take responsibility for the disrespect we show them. That's where decreasing disrespect and increasing gratitude at home requires a DIY effort. You're going to have to identify and take responsibility for your own disrespect.

Right now, are you aware of disrespectful attitudes or behaviors you've had toward your loved ones in recent days and weeks? Think about specific instances when you were critical, dismissive, or belittling in your verbal and nonverbal communication. What if someone had treated you that way, how would you have felt? How did your loved ones react? How do you think they felt?

It is time to apologize and ask for forgiveness. It will require humility and bravery on your part (two more good relationship tools). Then talk through ways in which you and they already show gratitude and could increase your efforts in this area. Seeing you decrease disrespect and increase gratitude, which in this case is the "it" in DIY, will be a good encouragement to your spouse and family. You can't fully control what they will or won't do, but you can always **do** more **yourself** as a way of cheering on your family toward home improvement goals.

"This was the hardest area of improvement for me," Kevin shared. "Where I grew up, you had to be tough to earn respect; you didn't go around telling people, 'Hey, I really appreciate you.' So, now as a husband and father, to turn things around at home, I had to develop a new kind of toughness—the kind that earns respect and demonstrates respect by being tender and expressing my gratitude for my family."

 ## ALL-IN BUDGET

To increase your odds of getting **all** your family **in** on decreasing disrespect and increasing gratitude, you might try a little experiment.

Consider your spouse and the good things that he or she does for you and your family. And consider your children and the laughter and joy they bring to your life. Yes, your spouse and children, like you, aren't perfect. Yes, they cause you some headaches now and then, as you do them. But when you focus more on the good than on the bad, you more easily realize just how much you have to be grateful for—a spouse and children who love you and who have far more good qualities than bad.

Now, clinging tightly to a grateful mindset, and resisting your "but what about . . ." excuses, try criticizing your spouse or children. See what I mean? It's more difficult to criticize, dismiss, or belittle your loved ones when you have a mindset of gratitude.

 ## SWEAT EQUITY

To move from experimental mode and lock in gratitude as your family's way of being with each other, keep the conversation going. That's what work crews (and families) do! They keep talking about the home improvement project, steadily working out the details as they put in the sweat equity to complete the job.

In chapter 2, we've explored the home improvement tool of gratitude. The following is a recap of important tips for decreasing disrespect and increasing gratitude:

- **Appreciate your spouse and children.** Keep your lists of gratitudes for each family member in a place where you can review it regularly. Seek to verbalize appreciation at least twice a week to each family member. When you feel disappointed or angry with a family member, ask for a time to sit down and share your concerns in a kind, caring manner.

- **Practice gentleness.** Even with our best efforts, disrespect is apt to still happen at least occasionally because we're imperfect humans. Yet families can learn to be assertive and gentle in our responses to each other. We don't have to worsen the situation by responding with our own forms of criticism, dismissiveness, and belittling.

- **Own your disrespect.** Don't be a better blamer of others than you are of yourself. Taking personal responsibility for your own disrespect frees you up to see the good in your family and gives you a new and improved perspective on your family members' disrespect. Plus, your family sees your humility and bravery and may be more apt to own their disrespect as well.
- **Walk all over floors, not your family.** Disrespect can really wear and tear on your relationships. Protect and preserve your relationships by valuing and caring for them like we value and care for new floors.
- **Build a sense of belonging.** You, your spouse, and your children want to believe and trust that you each belong in the family. Treating each other with gratitude and respect is an important way of saying, "You belong here! You're my people. I've got your back!"

 ## BIG REVEAL

A husband says to his wife, "I'm sorry I spoke to you that way. You didn't deserve that."

A wife says to her husband, "Thank you for all you do for our family. You sacrifice so much for us."

Instead of yelling at his younger brother and calling him names, an older brother says, "You made me really mad. I don't like it when you tear up my stuff."

Mom and Dad receive a handmade card from their kids that says "thank you for being awesome parents" and has a "help-around-the-house" coupon book in it.

These are snapshots of gratitude that warm our hearts as individuals, couples, and parents. But they are also "big reveal" moments—moments that don't happen without a plan, without some DIY, and without sweat equity.

As you continue with your home improvement efforts, keep looking for your own big reveal moments. While you're at it, keep looking for the good in each other and thanking each other for your little and big steps toward more gratitude and less disrespect. Change takes time, but when you're *all* in and all *in*, you're better able to enjoy the home improvements you're making together as a team.

TALK IT OVER

1. What qualities are you grateful for in your spouse? In your children? How do you and your family show gratitude toward each other?

2. Watch and listen to your kids this week. Which of their disrespectful attitudes and behaviors might they have picked up from you?

3. What was it like for you to grow up in either a respectful or disrespectful home?

4. At the end of the week, ask your spouse this question, "Have I done or said anything this week that discouraged you?" You might also ask the same question to your children.

HOME IMPROVEMENT GOAL:
Remove apathy.

HOME IMPROVEMENT TOOL:
Cultivate love.

Chapter 3

CULTIVATING LOVE

Love tears down walls!

#yougottalaugh

GARY: Karolyn is a great cook, and she's fluent in my love language—words of affirmation. She keeps my stomach and my love tank full! #Love is the answer!

SHANNON: I'm trying to love my husband and our kids really well so that they don't get any ideas about replacing me. #Love the ones you're with!

I'M ALWAYS AMAZED at how much open space home renovation experts create when they remove walls. They're not really adding square footage, but wow, removing walls makes you think and feel like you have more space. You somehow see that same space much differently than before.

Similarly, we improve our relationships and our home

life when we tear down the emotional walls we've put up between each other over time. For example, where there once was a wall of bitterness, a wall of jealousy, or a wall of mistrust, we now open up the space between us by working through our bitterness, jealousy, or mistrust in healthy ways.

Shannon and I both work with individuals and couples who have to demolish these more serious types of problems, or walls, to be able to restore and renew healthy relationships. But for many families, there is a much more common, much more easily removed wall of apathy that they must deal with if they and their loved ones are going to enjoy new and improved relationships.

Apathy simply means that we take each other for granted. We assume that our love for one another is unshakeable and that our relationships can thrive even when we fail to prioritize them. Unfortunately, I know many couples and families who have built walls of apathy at home. They didn't necessarily mean to, but by failing to convey love for one another, they essentially conveyed an apathetic, or an "I don't care," attitude.

My wife, Karolyn, and I dealt with apathy earlier in our marriage. I was in graduate school and working part-time. She was also working. We were busy, and I assumed all was well, but we were slowly drifting apart. We were focused on our work and studies and less and less focused on each other.

You, too, may have experienced marital drift. When we drift, we always drift apart. No matter how busy, we cannot afford to put our physical and emotional closeness on hold too long. When we do, our communication tends to decrease and misunderstandings increase. Our stress levels rise. We then blame one another for our stress. This common spiral of negative effects wears on us and can cause us to question our love for one another.

As one man said, "I knew we were having some problems, but I didn't realize how serious things were until my wife broke down crying in the counseling office. She said I didn't love her anymore. That was so far from the truth. I loved her more than ever, but I wasn't showing it clearly enough."

It's not just couples who sometimes feel unloved. In the busyness of life, parents can inadvertently take their children for granted. Shannon knows about this on a personal level.

"Avery and Carson call me out periodically for being on my cellphone when I should be listening to them. They have a way of laying it on thick, too. They'll say things like, 'Oh, I guess your cellphone is more important than I am.' Ouch!"

Shannon's sons did not mince words; they asked for and received the attention they needed. But in many cases, children can't express themselves. Children may then persist to the point of misbehaving to get their needs met, which is something Shannon also understands from a professional level.

"When a parent tells me their child is misbehaving, one of the first factors I wonder about is whether or not the child feels loved. I know their parents love them. But does the child feel loved? That's a much different question."

In addition to couples and children feeling the negative effects of being taken for granted, we need to acknowledge the hurt feelings siblings have when they take each other for granted. When this occurs, it is typically but not always that an older sibling refuses to play with or help a younger sibling. Of course, in fairness, older siblings sometimes feel that their younger siblings take their time and personal space for granted. These circumstances can definitely lead to a "love loss" between siblings.

If your family is dealing with walls of apathy at home, my encouragement to you is this: tear down those walls! To do that, add more love to your home improvement toolbox. By increasing love, you and your loved ones will be better able to open up what has become closed-off emotional space between you. No more shutting each other out! It's time to tear down those hurtful "I don't care" walls and begin seeing and treating each other with the love you all so desperately need and want.

LOVE: I'M WITH YOU AND FOR YOU

I see love much like the sledgehammer home renovators use when they demolish walls. Hammers remove walls like love removes the emotional walls that separate and distance us from one another.

Inside our walls of apathy is fear. We're afraid of being alone. I don't mean we're afraid of having a few minutes and hours to ourselves; I mean we want to know that someone is truly with us and for us in this life—someone who loves us deeply and with whom we can face and overcome life's challenges. Apathy causes us to doubt each other's love, and in turn, our fear of being alone and unloved rises.

We don't typically mean to be apathetic or uncaring. In fact, many people I work with think they are being loving. However, their loved ones feel unloved and uncared for. How can this be? How can one person think they're communicating love while the other person feels unloved? It's almost as if they're speaking two different languages!

> We want to know that someone is truly with us and for us in this life.

Karolyn and I encountered this miscommunication problem early in our marriage, and I recognized this same problem for so many other couples I counseled. From those experiences came my book *The 5 Love Languages: The Secret to Love That Lasts*, which has since sold millions of copies worldwide, demonstrating that people want and need to express heartfelt love to one another. Let me share a brief overview of the five love languages concept.

The five love languages are five ways to express love emotionally.

Words of Affirmation—The words may focus on how they look, something they did for you, their personality, or anything you admire about them.

Receiving Gifts—The gifts need not be expensive. The gift says, "They were thinking about me."

Quality Time—Giving the person your undivided attention. It may involve extended conversations or doing a project together.

Acts of Service—Doing something you know they would like for you to do, such as washing dishes, vacuuming the floors, or helping a child with a project.

Physical Touch—Hugs, kisses, high fives, etc.

Typically each of us has a primary love language. One of the five speaks more deeply to us than the others. By nature, we speak our own language. What makes me feel loved is what I do to show my love to others. However, that may not be the love language of the other person, so he or she may not feel loved even though I am loving them. Thus, many husbands and wives miss each other emotionally. Three questions will help you discover your love language:

1. How do I typically express love to others?

2. What do I complain about most often?

3. What do I request most often?

You may also take the free online profile at www.5love languages.com.

Knowing our own love language is a good starting place, but we also have to identify our loved ones' love languages. If they and we share the same primary love language, we'll have a little easier time expressing love to each other.

However, communicating love can be a bit more difficult if we don't speak the same love language. We have to exert more effort in learning and speaking our loved one's love language when that language is different from ours. For example, my love language is words of affirmation, and Karolyn's is acts of service. I do not like to vacuum floors, but I love Karolyn, so I vacuum floors as a way of showing her I love her. My failure to speak her love language would come across as apathy, or as me not caring about her. That's the last thing she or I want. So what do I do? I look for ways to serve her. My love language is words of affirmation. So she tells me how great I am. I wish we had known about the love languages when we were first married.

DRAWING UP THE PLANS

As you reflect on your own childhood, on a scale of 0 to 10, how much love did you feel coming from your mother? Your father? Which love language did your mother speak most often? Your father? Now that you understand the love language concept, does it help you understand why you did or did not feel loved by your parents?

I am rather certain that you love your own children. However, your love will become more effective if you understand the primary love language of your child. I would encourage you to have your child or teenager take the free online profile at www.5lovelanguages.com to help determine their love language.

I would like to encourage you to have another family time in which the entire family discusses the love language concept. Let each family member share with the family which love language they prefer.

In my books *The 5 Love Languages of Children* and *The 5 Love Languages of Teenagers*, I share the idea that each of us has an emotional love tank. One fun way to keep love alive in the family is to periodically ask a family member this question, "On a scale of 0 to 10, how full is your love tank?" If they say anything less than 10, you ask, "What could I do to help fill it?" They give you an idea, and you now have information that can help you effectively love your spouse and your children.

Of course, love has more characteristics than the five love languages. In all of literature, many agree that the clearest description of love is found in the New Testament book of 1 Corinthians, which reads as follows:

> Love is patient, love is kind. It does not envy, it does not boast, it is not proud. It does not dishonor others, it is not self-seeking, it is not easily angered, it keeps no record of wrongs. Love does not delight in evil but rejoices with the truth. It always protects, always trusts, always hopes, always perseveres.
>
> Love never fails . . .[1]

Imagine treating each other this way. In fact, why not let this be your family's blueprint for increasing love at home? The passage defines love in a clear and thorough way. There are no mixed messages, and there are no unrealistic conditions about what we should or shouldn't do to be loving. No! Instead, this classic statement brings together everything good we've ever learned about love. It stretches us to be our best to each other, and that is when love flourishes.

Perhaps you're thinking, "We'll never be able to pull that off!" Families think that same thought when they're contemplating making big changes to their houses. That's what R. J. and Jamie felt. "We were at our limits," Jamie recalled. "We were cold toward each other and growing apart, and I really felt like we couldn't rebound. But I guess that was our 'rock bottom.' R. J. and I started talking about what would happen to the children if we didn't get it together, and that's when we began to get way more serious about making changes."

Like R. J. and Jamie, if you really want change—if you're truly tired of taking each other for granted—then you've got to push yourselves for the reward of home improvement. I suppose you could say "no pain, no gain!"

Of course, you also need to keep in mind that no major renovation happens overnight. That's true of literal home improvement, and it's true for relationship and home life improvement. Consider the pursuit of love an ongoing project in which you'll sometimes succeed and sometimes fail. In time, as you and your family prioritize and commit to loving each other better, you'll see that you and they will succeed more than fail. And I venture to say you'll watch apathy nearly disappear because you are striving for such a high standard of love.

 ## DO-IT-YOURSELF

A crew is only as good as their leader! To motivate your family to get on board with loving each other better, you're going to need to step up your efforts. How will you stop taking your family for granted and start loving them more?

As your home improvement consultant, my recommendation is that you start by studying the five love languages concept and identifying your own love language. This investment of time and thought will open your eyes in a new way to what love means to you. Perhaps you previously would have felt frustrated by your spouse's neglect of your love tank and shut down. Now, you'll be better equipped to recognize what's happening and then verbalize your needs. As a physical touch love language person, for example, rather than passively sulk or aggressively criticize them, you might assertively ask for what you need: "Honey, I could really use a hug right now."

Your study of the five languages can also inspire you to consider your family's love languages in an all-new way. For example, you might catch yourself wishing your child would stop "nagging" you to play with her. By learning to view that child's request as an invitation to fill her "quality time" love tank, you'll be better able to show more patience with even the whiniest of attitudes because you know that's the only way she knows how to get the quality time she needs. "See" the tank, fill the tank! Lack of concern or attentiveness (apathy) will not fill her love tank; only love will.

"See" the tank, fill the tank!

You may be thinking, "But will anyone speak my love language?" That's a normal desire and, ultimately, a healthy request. You want your family to love you back. You'd actually like for them to initiate expressions of love so that you're not always the one responsible for initiating. In addition to assertively asking for what you need, you might also try noticing how your loved ones are trying to love you. Likely, they love you dearly and are expressing love in their primary love language. You just may be missing it either because you're not paying attention or because you don't speak their primary love language. This is where learning their love language will help you better detect when they're attempting to express their love for you.

These are just a few thoughts to help you do it yourself, or love better, before you expect your loved ones to love better. Seeing you in action will hopefully help motivate them to love better too.

ALL-IN BUDGET

A great starting place for getting ***all*** the family all ***in***, or on board, with loving each other better is to simply begin a conversation about love. I have several resources available to help you with these conversations, but you can simply ask each other two basic questions: 1) How do you know I love you? And 2) When most recently did you feel like I was loving toward you?

An important ground rule when asking these questions is that you and your loved ones not dispute what each other say. Shaming your loved one for their honesty or otherwise suggesting that they don't see your efforts at loving them will not decrease apathy. In fact, you may actually only add to the walls of apathy by further pushing your loved one away when you reject their thoughts and feelings. Instead, thank them for their honesty and let them know that you plan on doing a better a job at expressing your love for them.

As one mom shared, "It was hurtful at first to think that

my daughter didn't feel loved by me. But when I realized I hadn't been speaking her love language, I totally got it. I was expressing love in my own primary love language but not taking into account that she is a words of affirmation kid and didn't value my service as much as she did my reassurance and encouraging words."

In addition to talking about love, observe your family interactions. What do you see and hear? When you, as a family, experience each other being loving, say it! "You're speaking my language!" This is a fun way of motivating each other to look for and celebrate the good home improvement efforts you're making as a family.

It's also healthy for you and your family to express negative feelings. If you feel you're being taken for granted, you can and should say it. As Shannon says, her sons let her know if they feel she isn't attending to their love tank needs. She adds, "I try to honor their appropriate requests, and I help them 'edit' their inappropriate requests. There are times, for example, that I have to be on my cellphone for work-related matters. If they're snappy with me, I acknowledge their request but ask and thank them for their patience while I finish my work."

Shannon's point reminds us of some of the realities related to loving each other better. We're not always going to be able to affirm, spend time, give gifts, serve, and touch in exactly the way and at exactly the time our loved ones desire. However, we can typically do a much better job than we are currently by stepping up as a team and working together to love better.

SWEAT EQUITY

As you tear down the walls of apathy in your home life, I must warn you: You and your family stand to have fun in the process! I liken this to home renovators on "Demo Day." Demolition is hard work, but those construction teams are invested in and excited about creating open spaces. You and your team are opening up spaces of a different kind and using a fun and powerful tool—love! Get ready to watch those walls of apathy go flying!

To help you load your toolbox with more love, here is a recap on the tips I've shared with you in chapter 3. These insights and actions will require some hard work, but the sweat equity you'll be investing in to decrease apathy and increase love will be well worth it.

- **Set an apathy alarm.** We usually don't mean to take each other for granted, but apathy can sneak in before we realize it. By actively watching for signs that we're taking each other for granted, we help our families guard against apathy. We might even encourage and permit each other to say, "I feel like you're taking me for granted," or, "I feel like you don't care." Those types of statements are great "alarms" that can cue us to improve and increase our expressions of love for each other.

- **Know and speak the five love languages.** We love each other, but if we want our loved ones to know we love them, we need to speak their love language. Whatever their language is—words of affirmation, quality time, gifts, acts of service, or physical touch—we need to learn it and speak it. When we talk together about the love languages and actively work to implement this concept, our home life will improve. If we fail to fill our loved ones' love tanks, our home life will continue to experience the emotional separation and distance caused by our walls of apathy.

- **Notice!** Pay attention to how your loved ones are asking you to fill their love tank. And pay attention to how they're trying to fill your love tank. We're sometimes naturally speaking our own love language and fail to correctly interpret others' love languages. We can be critical of each other when, instead, we should be more appreciative of each other's efforts. Viewing love through a five love languages lens will help us better appreciate and encourage each other in our efforts to express and experience more love at home.

- **Be assertive.** We need to first love each family member well. We don't need to expect them to do more than we're doing in this area of home improvement. However, we also want to enjoy a full love tank, and sometimes need to be more assertive in asking for what we need. Passiveness won't get the job done, nor will aggressiveness. Assertiveness is the way to go.

- **Persist.** We often tend to give up too easily. In the case of love, we want a little to go a long way, when really, our loved ones need and want more frequent expressions of love. The more we persist, the more they feel loved. However, sometimes we've neglected our loved ones for so long that they are mistrustful or resentful toward our new-and-improved persistence. Our persistence will become even more important under these circumstances. We should remain hopeful that, little by little, our persistence will pay off, and the walls between us will come down.

- **Be selective.** Definitions and demonstrations of love abound, yet all are not equally healthy and good. Society is full of mixed messages about what love is and is not. Consider 1 Corinthians 13:4–8 as your go-to blueprint for cultivating love and removing walls of apathy between you and your loved ones.

 ## BIG REVEAL

When we start either kind of home improvement project, literal or relational, we don't always know what we're getting ourselves into. We have a plan, and we're committed to it, but we won't know the end result until we can actually see it to believe it.

Karolyn and I didn't know what to expect early in our marriage. We were committed to each other but drifting apart rather than drawing closer to one another. One of our big reveal moments happened when I finally got honest with God and prayed, "God, I don't know what else to do to love Karolyn. I've tried everything I know." Following His lead, I asked her how I could love her better, and she told me. I began speaking her love language (even though I would not have used that term). She began speaking mine. And little by little, the walls between us began coming down—and have stayed down—because of our ongoing, intentional efforts to love each other better.

When your family's walls of apathy come down, what might your big reveal look like? Imagine how you might see and appreciate each other differently. Imagine how it will feel to not take each other for granted but instead, to love and care for each other by keeping the love tank full.

The prospects for change are exciting! Life is too short to wait any longer to love each other better. Do it today, while you can!

TALK IT OVER

1. What expression(s) of love do you most prefer—words of affirmation, quality time, gifts, acts of service, or physical touch? Ask your spouse and/or children (if they're old enough to understand) what they think their primary love language is. See if they can guess yours.

2. How in the last week have you expressed love toward your spouse and/or children? Were you speaking your love language or theirs?

3. How in the last week have your spouse or children expressed love toward you? Were they speaking their love language or yours?

4. In what ways might your children sometimes be misbehaving when they are actually trying to get their love tanks filled?

5. Identify some examples of how you and your family have taken each other for granted lately. What is one step you and they could take to turn that around?

HOME IMPROVEMENT GOAL:
Negotiate conflict.

HOME IMPROVEMENT TOOL:
Seek compromise.

Chapter 4

SEEKING COMPROMISE

We can afford to disagree on colors, carpets, fixtures, and faucets, but we need to agree to "decorate" our homes with peace and harmony. They never go out of style!

#yougottalaugh

GARY: When one of us wins, we all win . . . unless, of course, the "one" is always you. #Compromise for the win!

SHANNON: "It's my way or the highway" never really works out unless you're somebody who just really likes a lot of lonely "highway" time. #Compromise or bust!

FAMILY LIFE is full of differences of opinion. For example, you want your child to wear the blue pants; she is set on wearing the purple pants. Your spouse believes washing and waxing the car is a top priority; you need him to run errands. Your parents want the whole family to vacation together for a full week in the mountains; you're in for a family vacation as long as it's not a full week and anywhere but the mountains.

Similarly, differences of opinion often flare when it comes to decorating our homes. You want more of an industrial look; your spouse loves the rustic look. Or you're all about getting rid of an old, worn-out recliner, but your spouse says, "No way, I just got that thing broke in good!"

Then there are your children. Your teenage son wants to decorate his room with Star Wars posters; you're good with one wall being Star Wars, but "Really, the whole room?" Your younger son thought it would be a good idea to paint one of his walls with some finger paints while you were on the phone. Your response, "Yes, I told you we could paint your wall. We. Not you. And not with finger paints."

Differences in opinion such as these can quickly erupt into full-blown conflict. You know . . . that tug-of-war tension we feel when we both want our way. We naturally want to win, so we "pull" a little harder on our end of that imaginary rope by pleading and bargaining. We sometimes try to bypass conflict by going ahead with our desires rather than consult with the other person (an "ask for forgiveness later" strategy). Or in moments of near defeat, we may go the passive-aggressive route in hopes that we can guilt the other person into letting go of their end of the tug-of-war rope. "Fine, have it your way!"

If we get our way, we think, "Great, all is well!" If we

don't get our way, we can build negative feelings toward one another. "You don't understand." "You don't care about my feelings." "You always have to win." You don't like to feel like this, and as importantly, neither do your loved ones.

Interior designers experience these types of conflicts when attempting to design comfortable spaces that reflect the styles and interests of each family member. That's why they ask so many questions about the family—ages, stages, favorite colors, preferred textures, favorite things, etc. With this information, they're better able to make design choices that match the family's unique style.

This same approach is true for the do-it-yourselfers among us. We want to update and customize our homes in ways that make all the family happy and comfortable, but that's easier said than done. As Shannon told me, "I want our home to be a family-friendly place where the kids can play, but I also don't want their stuff all over the place. Finding the good middle ground can be tricky."

Differences over how a family decorates their home is hardly the most heated conflict a couple will ever experience, of course. Some of you *wish* that was the only thing you fight about. Try: differences in parenting/discipline approaches; differences in time management patterns; differences in money-management styles; differences in how much in-law involvement is preferred; and differences in religious beliefs and practices. These types of conflict, if left unresolved, can kindle long-term problems for couples.

Like couples, parents and children also experience intense conflict around subjects like bedtime and curfew, screen time, fair punishment, and communication break-downs. We may think, "Parents call the shots; kids should do what the parents say." Yes, that may be true, but as the child gets older their opinions need to be heard. Treat them as the person they are. Sure, parents have the final decision based on what they think best for the child.

Ongoing patterns of conflict tend to be a home improvement issue that I see a lot of in my work with people. Many couples and parents want to live with less strife and more peace and harmony at home. As their "home improvement" helper, I first encourage them to put the imaginary tug-of-war rope down. Let's stop fighting. We are on the same team.

Not all differences of opinion result in conflicts. He likes salmon. She prefers chicken. His favorite color is green; hers is purple. These are not conflicts, but simply personal preferences. Conflicts arise in a family relationship when two family members disagree on an issue and insist that their view is the best view. A conflict is usually accompanied by strong emotions—often with anger.

We don't ask for conflicts. They just appear in the normal flow of life. It is a perfectly lovely evening until she says, "I would really like for us to go to my folks for Christmas this year." To which he responds, "Honey, I really don't think I can take that for five days." They have just encountered a conflict.

Conflict is inevitable simply because we are humans. We have different thoughts, feelings, preferences and opinions. The key to family harmony is learning to negotiate conflicts without damaging our relationship. This is where the home improvement tool of compromise is so helpful.

WHY COMPROMISE?

"I'm tired of fighting." This statement is one that Shannon and I frequently hear in counseling. That sentiment is also a top reason people are willing, or should be willing, to consider compromise as a valuable home improvement tool. If you're tired of fighting, at some point you have to learn to compromise.

Compromise can mean finding some middle ground between ourselves and the other person. That could be an exact "middle," in which both sides compromise an equal amount. For example, for the couple who is in conflict about which family to spend the holidays with, a 50/50 compromise may be that the two sets of in-laws rotate coming for Thanksgiving and Christmas each year so that each set would come for at least one of the two holidays each year. Or we may visit them on a rotating basis.

Compromise can also mean less than a 50/50 agreement. For example, a teenage daughter wants to download music through a popular app. Her mother is willing to allow that but only under her supervision, with her also checking periodically to ask her daughter about her music and talk about the lyrics of various songs. This way, rather than telling the daughter no to downloads, the mother is allowing her some but not full freedom.

Put yourself in these situations. In both, you are still technically getting your way while also allowing the other person to get their way. You're also potentially eliminating fighting about the conflict by clearly establishing what the new understanding is. I say "potentially eliminating the fighting" because compromise is not only about finding and agreeing to uphold a new middle ground; compromise is also about attitude change. If we want peace and harmony, we need to have a peaceful, harmonious attitude as opposed to a contentious attitude that contributes to conflict and fighting. In compromise we are looking for a win-win solution. Contrast compromise with arguing. In an argument, you are each trying to get your way. If you win the argument, the other person lost. It is no fun to live with a loser, so why create one? Remember, we are on the same team.

Attitude is generally a major influence on how we process conflict. I like Shannon's perspective. "We can see conflict as a pest, or a step. Yes, conflict can be an annoyance, or pest. But it can also be a step that propels us in our understanding of each other, and our ability to partner together as a team."

P.E.S.T.	S.T.E.P.
Patience—Low	Style—Open to Compromise
Expectations—My Way	Treatment of Other Person—Loving
Style—Argumentative	Expectation—Our Way
Treatment of Other Person—Harsh	Patience—High

A positive attitude that respects the value of the other person makes compromise possible.

You and I both know that some matters cannot be compromised. Safety matters, matters related to trust in the marriage or trust between a parent and child, and certain religious convictions are a few areas in which compromise is not the answer. There may also be resentment (chapter 5) and anger (chapter 9) that needs to be dealt with before compromise may be possible. Remember that in harder situations, you may need the support of a professional counselor to help you work through more serious home improvement changes.

 ## DRAWING UP THE PLANS

When you choose to seek compromise rather than arguing, there are three possible types of compromise. After respectfully listening to each other, and asking, "How can we solve our conflict?" you need to explore these three.

  1. I will move to your side.

      Husband >>>>>>>> | <<<<<<<< Wife

One of you agrees that on this issue, you are willing to go with their idea.

  2. I will meet you in the middle.

      Husband >>>>>>>> | <<<<<<<< Wife

This is the 50/50 compromise we discussed earlier.

3. I will meet you later.

Husband >>>>>>>> | <<<<<<<< Wife

We really cannot come to a solution at the moment. So let's agree to disagree and perhaps visit this again later. In the meantime, we will love and care for each other.

Sometimes this form of compromise can be a permanent solution. The toothpaste conflict—middle or bottom squeezer? We agree to get two tubes of toothpaste.

Allow yourself for a moment to consider how compromise might create or add to the home makeover you're hoping for. Can you imagine it? Perhaps in your imagined blueprint, your eight-year-old accepts your compromise—she can wear one of three options to school, but she can't wear the one item she's been bugging you to wear. Or maybe your spouse accepts your compromise—he is willing to cut back on keeping junk-food snacks at home if you will not nag him when he occasionally overdoes it at the buffet table at a social or church function. Another possibility for your new and improved home life may feature you accepting your sixteen-year-old's request for more freedom by extending his curfew by one hour on Friday nights. Or it could be that, at your spouse's request, you finally agree as your act of compromise to be kinder to your mother-in-law even though you don't always see eye to eye with her.

I share these examples with you because they are common examples of compromise in our work with couples and families. You have your own needs for compromise.

What are they? Before you can even find the middle ground between yourself and your spouse, child, or other family members, what attitude changes will *you* need to make to further commit to peace and harmony at home?

One couple I worked with decided together that they would both give up one of their extracurricular activities so that they could have a set date night each week. This was a mutual compromise that required letting some others down so that they could stop letting each other down. I saw them months later, and they shared that their once-a-week date night had done wonders for their marriage.

Another couple I worked with found a way of sharing family responsibilities in the mornings and evenings so that both people felt supported. Before they had children, they could leave for work or come home from work as they pleased. As they grew their family, however, morning and evening routines required "all hands on deck," or else one parent would end up feeling overwhelmed. To adjust, the couple figured out a reasonable balance such that she was still able to get in her early morning exercise because he helped make breakfast, pack lunches, and dress the children; and he still worked a little later a couple days a week because she took over after-school pickup and dinner-making duties on those days.

Both of these couples made attitude changes. They went from prioritizing their own interests and needs to prioritizing their needs as a couple. Because of their attitude change, peace and harmony between them increased, and that, in turn, helped them to find the middle ground their marriage needed to thrive.

As you're envisioning what your remodeled home life might look like with more compromise, remember, we can't avoid conflict, but we can adjust our reaction to conflict. We can adopt a more peaceful, harmonious attitude, and we can see conflict as a step toward positive change as opposed to a purposeless pest.

 ## DO-IT-YOURSELF

Some people are naturally good at compromise. They may have grown up with positive role models who demonstrated healthy compromise habits, or they may have learned through their own trial and error that compromise was the way to go. Other people compromise too much, meaning they give everyone else their way simply to avoid an argument. Still other people rarely compromise. They're more of the "my way or the highway" kind of people.

How are you at compromise? Are you doing well and don't need to make any changes? If so, congratulations on already having the tool of compromise in your relationship toolbox! Make that work for you as you lead your family in the art of compromise.

If you need to step up your efforts at compromise, what will you do to take action? As you already know, we have to be assertive with our home improvement efforts—it is truly a do-it-yourself project. Why? Because, unlike installing new carpet, we can't hire someone else to come in and change our attitude or cause us to view conflict as a step rather than a pest—we have to do this work for ourselves.

ALL-IN BUDGET

One way of getting ***all*** the family to go all ***in*** on compromise is to agree as a family to call a time-out during times of conflict. Anyone could call the time-out. After the time-out, the next step would be for each person involved in the conflict to calmly say how they feel in that moment. Together, they would then talk about some possible options for resolving the conflict as a team.

"I've got to tell you, I am all for telling our kids to calm down and take a time-out," Mikayla told Shannon, "but I'm not buying that this will work. You don't know our kids! For that matter, I don't even know if Ben and I can realistically remain that calm under pressure."

Like Mikayla and Ben, most families have to prepare for these types of time-outs. Families should talk in advance about their commitment to each other, their desire to continue growing as a team, and their desire to support one another even when they have differences of opinion. Parents can choose kid-friendly terms to explain this concept to younger children. In some cases, parents may simply quietly commit to a more peaceful, harmonious approach to conflict and then call time-outs as needed without any advance explanation to the children.

If you, as an adult, don't commit to peace and harmony,

> You've got to practice what you preach, in easy and hard moments of conflict.

you may not gain much traction with time-outs and positive talk. You've got to practice what you preach, in easy and hard moments of conflict. The hard moments will be especially difficult for a while, but you can and should continue to reiterate to your spouse, children, or other family members that you are committed to peace and harmony and want to work together to find peaceful solutions to conflicts.

As always, when you and your loved ones successfully use a home improvement tool such as compromise, notice and celebrate that as an important accomplishment. When you or they miss the target, call it out, but stay positive. "Well guys, we blew it. But we'll keep trying."

You should also be especially encouraging of your children when they accept your decisions. They don't have to be happy about all your decisions, but they hopefully can see and hear in your rules that you care about their safety and their ability to appropriately comply with authority. As they age and grow in responsibility and wisdom, you will be able to give them reasonable freedoms. You may at times get tired of explaining these things to them, but in the long run, you'll be glad you stayed at it, as will they.

SWEAT EQUITY

Increasing compromise to resolve conflict is going to require some serious sweat equity. That's why couples and families get into trouble with conflict in the first place—it's sometimes seems easier to fight for our way than to work toward peaceful outcomes that are in our and the other person's best interest. But ultimately, if we want peace and harmony, we have to be willing to put in the time and work needed to find a middle ground wherever possible.

In chapter 4, we've explored the home improvement tool of compromise. The following is a recap of important tips for defusing conflict and increasing compromise:

- **Put down the tug-of-war rope.** Differences in opinion are a fact of life. We know this, but somehow, we pull against one another as if differences in opinion are not okay. Remember that differences in opinion and conflict are, in fact, permissible and even productive if we handle them in a healthy manner. After all, we're on the same team!

- **Compromise for the win!** Look for opportunities to allow your loved ones to voice their opinions and get their way. For example, it probably doesn't matter if your daughter wears the blue pants or the purple pants as long as she has pants on. Or if you're husband loves his worn-out recliner, either have it reupholstered or throw a blanket over it to help it blend with your other new furniture; let him keep his recliner. In both instances, you and the other person both win because you valued their opinion and allowed them to have their way rather than pushing harder for yours.

- **All middle grounds are not equal.** Sometimes you and your loved ones will be able to negotiate a 50/50 balanced compromise; other times, someone may have to give more than someone else. Hopefully, as equals in the home, you and your spouse consistently find ways of honoring each other's preferences. With children, you may not always be able to arrive at a mutually agreeable "middle ground" because they are not developmentally ready for some of the freedoms they may petition for. In these situations, you, as the parent, have authority, and in your child's best interest, you may be able to allow some freedom of choice and/or independence but ultimately have to err on the side of caution.

- **Change your attitude.** If you want peace and harmony at home, you need to have a peaceful, harmonious attitude as opposed to a contentious mindset that contributes to conflict and fighting. Hopefully, your peaceful attitude is contagious and is "caught" by the others in the family.

- **See conflict as a "step" instead of a "pest."** Few of us enjoy conflict and instead see it as an annoyance, or a pest. But when we view conflict as a step toward positive change, then that can positively influence how we handle conflict. We can talk about this with our loved ones so that we're all thinking more about how to grow together through conflict.

- **Compromise starts with you!** We can't always wait on the other person to take the lead. Instead, we have to continually improve our use of compromise so that we're modeling for and encouraging others in the family to do the same.

- **Take a time-out.** To get you and your family in the habit of compromise, catch yourselves in moments of conflict, call a time-out, and then discuss what's happening, and work together as a team to resolve the conflict in a peaceful way. And, yes, practice makes perfect. Your family will have more of whatever it practices—conflict or compromise.

 ## BIG REVEAL

Aside from "I love you," and "I'm sorry," some of the most welcomed words we hear from each other as a couple or family are, "Okay, I will." Of course, the tone in which these words are said make a big difference. But when said in a peaceful way, they convey agreement. That's what we're looking for in our home life—agreement. Agreement isn't always easy to come by because differences of opinion easily turn to conflict if not handled well. But if we adopt peaceful, harmonious attitudes and learn to seek compromise when possible, we will tend to experience less conflict, and that's what so many couples and families want.

You and your family are embarking on major home

improvements right now. It's hard but valuable work. Keep moving forward!

TALK IT OVER

1. How did your family handle conflict when you were growing up?

2. What are some of your strengths and challenges when it comes to handling conflict?

3. What are some conflicts that you and your spouse have worked through?

4. What are typical conflicts between you and your children? How are you and they handling conflict together in positive ways?

5. How might you explain a conflict time-out to your kids? How do you think they'll react?

HOME IMPROVEMENT GOAL:
Reduce resentment.

HOME IMPROVEMENT TOOL:
Choose forgiveness.

Chapter 5

CHOOSING FORGIVENESS

Termite-free and grudge-free is the way to go if we want our houses and our home life to stand the test of time.

#yougottalaugh

GARY: "Forgiveness leads to happily ever after"—that's been my and Karolyn's goal all along. Thankfully, I've not needed as much forgiveness as she (don't tell her I said that)! #Forgiveness makes the heart grow fonder.

SHANNON: My kids act just like me, which means they need a lot of forgiveness! #Forgiveness is the best payback of all.

RESENTMENT IS A STRONG WORD. It's close in meaning to hatred and often involves long-standing bitterness, or grudge holding, because of a wrong we feel has been done to us.

A few of you just read that definition and think, "That's not our home. I'll just skim this chapter and move on." But I've found as a counselor that more homes are wrecked by resentment than you might expect.

In fact, resentment sometimes sneaks into our relationships before we're even aware it's happening. And then, after time passes, we more clearly see and feel the damage it leaves in its wake.

Termites and other wood-destroying pests do the same thing. They set in unnoticed and steadily damage the foundation of our houses. Water damage and ground settling have a similar effect—they all in time can cause shifts in our foundation, which can lead to uneven floors, cracks in the walls, and doors and windows that don't shut quite right. Those are visible effects of literal foundation damage.

> Resentment sneaks into our relationships before we're even aware it's happening.

But what does resentment "look" like, or better yet, sound like in our home lives?

"Sure, you'll finish remodeling our bathroom right after you finish building the shed out back—the one you started a year ago. I won't hold my breath."

"Work is your top priority. Everyone else gets the best you. Me? I get the tired you, the empty promises you."

"You never notice how clean the house is, that there are groceries in the refrigerator and food on the table, that the kids have their homework done. You think all that gets done by itself. No, I do it all. Me. With little to no help from you!"

"Once again, you side with your mother rather than me. Why am I not surprised?"

"You're always checking my texts and asking me where I've been. I've proven myself over and over. Can't you let the past be in the past?"

These resentful comments reveal the tension and "cracks" in the foundation of these couples' relationships. They reflect the hurt these people feel—the hurt that has set in over time, perhaps unnoticed early on, but then having grown so much that the couples now feel almost constant disdain for one another.

"I RESENT YOU BECAUSE YOU RESENT ME"

Like couples, parents and children also feel resentment toward each other. Parents don't like to admit this, but it's true. They sometimes subtly or not so subtly resent their kids because of the time and energy they require and how this can derail the parent's career and life goals. Some children are more difficult to rear, due to developmental delays, medical problems, or personality clashes between them and one or both parents. Sometimes children don't live up to their parents' expectations. This can contribute to the resentment in parents.

Children sense how their parents feel toward them and

respond accordingly. They often experience their own resentful feelings from not being loved unconditionally or not being given the time and energy they so desperately need and want.

Children may feel resentment toward their siblings as well when they perceive the other sibling as more favored by their parents or as generally better than them in various ways (e.g., smarter, more artistic, more athletic, more popular). Siblings also can dominate or even hurt each other emotionally and physically, and this, too, can lead to resentment.

Hurt, disappointment, and disillusionment are common features in all of the examples I've just shared. One person is hurt, disappointed by, or disillusioned with past and/or current treatment and blames the other person as the cause of their feelings. These conditions—both the resentment-provoking behaviors and the feelings of resentment—weaken family members' sense of connection or closeness.

Family members may express their resentment differently. Sometimes family members are ashamed of their resentment or otherwise don't want to face it. They quietly tuck those feelings away in their hearts and minds, but resentment left inside will eventually lead to an emotional explosion. Some won't talk about their hard feelings with their family but will talk to friends about how badly they are treated at home. Others will peacefully address their resentment with another family member, requesting change. Still others will confront a family member, demanding change. (None of us respond well to demands.) Young children typically aren't able to communicate their feelings with words but may do so through aggressive behavior.

If left unresolved, resentment by one family member can trigger a cycle of resentment. "I resent you because . . ." elicits a reaction of "I resent you because you resent me." That's all the more reason we as families need to learn to deal faster and more assertively with resentment. To do that, we need the home improvement tool of forgiveness.

AN ATTITUDE OF ACCEPTANCE

Corrie ten Boom knew firsthand the freedom that comes through forgiveness. She and her family were imprisoned in a Nazi concentration camp for hiding and aiding Jews during World War II. She later forgave Nazi soldiers for their cruelty because she felt morally convicted that she could not live forgiven and free unless she forgave and granted freedom to others who had done wrong to her. She said, "Forgiveness is the key that unlocks the door of resentment and the handcuffs of hatred."[1]

Our resentment of a family member does not imprison that person; our resentment imprisons us. It separates us physically and emotionally from our families. Resentment creates distance between us and our loved ones, which is the exact opposite of what we really want—closeness and connection. The good news is we also have the power to unlock the jail cell and shake free from our chains . . . when we forgive others.

It has been said that "a happy marriage is the union of two good forgivers."[2] I like that! I would add, a happy family is founded in forgiveness and always stands ready to forgive.

We have to learn to forgive happily ever after if we want to live happily ever after.

> Often we resent the fact that our spouse does not do things our way.

Not one of us is perfect. We will fail each other in little and big ways. Accepting this reality is an important starting place for cultivating a spirit of forgiveness at home.

In practical terms, we first choose an attitude of forgiveness when faced with the "small stuff." I call this "forbearance" or patience with the things that bug us about the other person. I'm talking about the way they leave hairs in the bathroom sink, the fact that they fail to hang up their clothes, or the way they load the dishwasher. It should be easy to overlook the small stuff in life, right? No, it's not easy. Often we resent the fact that our spouse does not do things our way.

So how do we handle the small stuff? I have a three-step plan that has helped many couples. Most couples can agree that they are irritated by certain things their spouse does, or fails to do. So let's agree that we would like to find a positive way to process these irritations.

First, each of you agrees that you will be open to a "request for change" every other week. So your spouse will make a request this week, and you will make a request next week. (That's twenty-six requests each year. That ought to be enough. Look at it this way—if you could get twenty-six things changed this year, would it be a good year for you?)

Second, before you make your "request for change," tell your spouse three things you like about them. For example: "I appreciate the fact that you always put your shoes in the closet." "I love the fact that you fix my coffee in the morning." "I really feel valued when you tell me that you love me."

Third, you share your request. "One of the things that would make my life easier would be if you would get the hairs out of the sink before you leave the bathroom." The other responds, "I'll try to work on that."

Once you have made your request, don't mention it again for at least three months. Give them time to change. Will they change everything? No! Will they change some things? Yes.

What do you do about the things they do not change? You "forbear." You cut them some slack. You accept their imperfections—those things they cannot or will not change. You must accept each other's humanity. No one will ever do everything the way you want it done. (This includes your children.)

The wise person chooses an attitude of acceptance, letting it go, refusing to let it divide you. We accept each other with our imperfections. We do not allow resentment to build up in our hearts. We choose to release those feelings and replace them with an attitude of love. "I will love you in spite of the fact that you continue to misplace your car keys every three days." Don't sweat the small stuff.

THE BIG STUFF: APOLOGIZING AND FORGIVING

However, what about the "big stuff"? I'm talking about harsh, unkind words, failing to speak your spouse's love language, putting time with your friends over time with your spouse, and refusing to listen to the other person's perspective when you have a conflict.

What do you do when your spouse has truly been unkind to you? Let's first of all admit that it will happen. None of us is perfect. We all experience anger and sometimes in anger say hurtful things. We don't have to be perfect to have a good marriage or be a good parent. But we do have to deal effectively with our failures. That involves apologizing and forgiving. There can be no long-term healthy marriages without apology and forgiveness.

What is the "big stuff" your family is dealing with? How has it gotten out of hand over time? Think about what issues you and your family argue most over or feel the most tension around. That's likely your "big stuff," or the big problems at the source of your relational foundation troubles.

Much like a home renovator, or perhaps in this case, a structural engineer, you have to investigate your foundation to determine just how bad the damage is. Then you can know how to best begin repairing and shoring up those supports.

May I suggest the best place to begin? Apologize for your part of the problem. Don't sit around waiting for your spouse to apologize. Maybe you think they are ninety-five percent of the problem, and your failure is only five percent.

Then deal with your five percent. Once you acknowledge your own failures, you make it easier for your spouse to apologize.

Let me also encourage you to apologize to your children when your behavior or words are not kind. They know that such behavior is not right. When you apologize, you keep them from building up resentment toward you.

When you apologize, the other person may say, "I will forgive you if you will forgive me." Wouldn't that be nice? That opens the door to true reconciliation. However, they may say, "I'll have to think about that." They may need some time to process their own feelings of hurt and resentment. Don't pressure them to forgive you. Forgiveness is a choice. Give them time to respond.

If your spouse apologized to you, I hope you will be quick to forgive. Forgiveness means you will lift the penalty, let go of resentment, and seek to move forward in the relationship. Inevitably, and understandably, when I teach on forgiveness, I get these questions: "What if he or she won't change? They apologize, but then continue doing the things that cause me to resent them."

That is a valid question that sometimes calls for "tough love." This is especially true in cases where a spouse is being abusive, dishonest, or disloyal, or where parents are dealing with rebellious teenage or young adult children. In challenging, often heartbreaking situations such as these, people need to use their best wisdom and consult with professionals to determine how to set healthy boundaries. Without boundaries, we tend to go on experiencing the same negative behaviors, which in turn, makes it difficult for us to decrease resentment and increase forgiveness. With boundaries, we send a clear message to our loved ones that certain behaviors won't be and can't be tolerated. Hopefully, they will then do their part to make change and mend the damage they have caused. All of this all takes time and effort. As in the case with more severe foundation damage, these situations may require the help of a trained counselor.

We must accept the reality that harboring resentment is not going to bring change. Apology and forgiveness is a much more powerful home improvement tool that will bring the change we long for.

 # DRAWING UP THE PLANS

Let's begin by asking the question: "What am I doing that hurts my spouse and causes them to resent me?" Perhaps they've already told you many times. Or perhaps you could ask them, "In what ways have I hurt you?"

As you're assessing the damage you've caused, you first have to decide how serious you are about repairing the damage. Since you're reading this book, I'm guessing you're serious. If so, your blueprint for change needs to involve genuine ownership of your damaging behaviors. Your loved ones are going to need to see and, more importantly, truly feel that you are remorseful. With that as your heart's desire, you're ready to express a long-overdue, heartfelt apology, but simply saying "I'm sorry" won't be enough.

Dr. Jennifer Thomas and I coauthored a book titled *When Sorry Isn't Enough.*[3] In that book, we talk about five unique expressions of apology.

1) Expressing regret—"I'm sorry for the times I have raised my voice and yelled at you." Tell them what you are sorry for, and never add the words, "but if you had not . . . then I would not . . ." Now you are no longer apologizing. You are blaming them for your poor behavior. "I know I've hurt you, and I deeply regret that."

2) Accepting responsibility—"I was wrong. I should not have done that. There is no excuse for what I did. I accept full responsibility."

3) Making restitution—"What can I do to make this up to you or to make this right?"

4) Expressing the desire to change—"I don't want to do that again. Can you help me find a way that I will not do that again?"

5) Requesting forgiveness—"Will you please forgive me?" Or, "I hope you can find it in your heart to forgive me. I love you."

So many times people say, "I just don't believe he or she is truly remorseful." Why do they say this? Because "I'm sorry" does not communicate sincerity. Most of us are willing to forgive if we believe the other person is sincere. We judge sincerity by the way they apologize. These five ways of expressing an apology will help you apologize sincerely. If you really want to see the relationship enhanced, humble yourself and fully apologize. If you do, watch the home improvements begin! (For further help in this area, go to www.5lovelanguages.com and take the free apology profile.)

Now, if you're someone who is withholding forgiveness, you, too, have to make some plans. Are you satisfied staying stuck in the resentment/unforgiveness mode, or are you ready to take a risk? I say "risk" because forgiveness is risky. You're basically saying to your loved one, "I know you're not perfect. I'm scared you'll hurt me again. But I officially release you from the resentment I've had toward you—I forgive you." Whew—that's a major relationship repair all in itself! In that big move, you've shored up a once cracked and broken connection in your relationship. You're hopeful the other person will see and feel that support and join you in mending the foundation of your home life, but you'll at least be doing your part.

DO-IT-YOURSELF

Doing your part! Easier said than done, isn't it? We want change, but we want others to change before *we* change.

As with all home improvement projects, to decrease resentment and increase forgiveness at home, you are going to have to do it yourself! That's right . . . you have to identify your part in the problem and then get to work on yourself before expecting change in others. If you're causing the resentment—after you apologize, commit in your heart to change your behavior. Change a little more every day until one day, you're truly a new and improved person. If you're harboring resentment—commit in your heart to forgive, then work on changing your own behavior. Little by little you can become the person you want to be.

You may be willing but afraid to change. Your fear is real and valid. To admit that we need to make change requires honesty, and makes us feel vulnerable. What if you didn't grow up in a home where apologies were encouraged? What if you admit failure and the other person doesn't forgive? You will have the freedom of knowing you have taken the first step. The ball is now in their court. On the other hand, what if you forgive, but their behavior continues to be hurtful? Then lovingly confront them with reality and request change. You may need to apply "tough love," but don't live with resentment. Release them to God; release your resentment to God. Life is too short to live with resentment. We either forgive if they apologize, or release them to God if they don't apologize. Either way, we are free to face the future with a positive spirit.

Our challenge is, if you need to forgive, you'll forgive; if you need to stop your hurtful behaviors, you stop your hurtful behaviors. It may not all happen overnight, but you've got to start somewhere! Why not right now?

ALL-IN BUDGET

Becoming a forgiving family is going to take everyone working together. Consistency in dealing with our failures and forgiving each other will restore a positive emotional climate in your family.

To get everyone on board, I recommend that you start with a family conference. You might say to your family, "I know that none of us is perfect. Sometimes I know that you children have heard me speak loudly to your mother/dad. That is not right. I have asked mom/dad to forgive me and they have. I know that sometimes I have lost my temper and spoken harshly to you children. That is wrong, and today I'm asking you to forgive me for that. I want you children to also learn to apologize when you say or do hurtful things to each other, or to mom/dad. I want our family to learn how to apologize and forgive each other. If you think I need to apologize, I give you permission to say, 'Mom/Dad, I think you need to apologize.' So let's learn to be a forgiving family, okay?" Chances are your family will get on board.

You might then ask each family member to make a list of the things other family members have done to hurt them and a list of the things they have said and done that hurt other family members. Then provide a time when each person can read their lists to the rest of the family. Then we can express forgiveness to each other. I call this a family forgiveness party. It can be the beginning of a new day in your family relationships.

> Forgiveness does not remove the memory, but it does free us to make the future better.

Asking for and giving forgiveness are both equally freeing. This doesn't mean that we instantly forget the past hurt or wrongdoing, but it's a start in the right direction. Forgiveness does not remove the memory, but it does free us to make the future better.

Make your home a no-grudge zone. You will no longer hold grudges against one another; instead, you will accept your own imperfections, and in doing so, accept your loved ones' imperfections. You and they can, and should, still work together to improve specific behaviors that have caused problems in the home. You might even need to hire a home improvement expert (a.k.a. family counselor) to help and hold you accountable to change, but if change is what you need, then now, not later, is the time to make change.

"Before we can teach our children to genuinely forgive each other, Sam and I have to learn to do the same thing," Ellen said to Sam and me in an early counseling session together. She and Sam both teared up as she talked because they both had felt the pain of harboring resentment toward each other. They and I knew they had a lot of work to do, but by seeking out counseling, they were off to a strong start.

 ## SWEAT EQUITY

If you've known the healing power of forgiveness, then you know forgiveness is worth the acceptance, vulnerability, and hard work it requires. If you've not known the healing power of forgiveness, then you may be skeptical. Either way, to experience freedom from resentment and restore the foundation damage resentment creates in our relationships, you and your family are going to need to practice forgiveness every day until it's a natural part of your home life.

We can't repair damage if we don't know about it.

In chapter 5, we've explored the home improvement tool of forgiveness. The following is a recap of important tips for decreasing resentment and increasing forgiveness:

- **Pay attention!** Shifts happen gradually in our foundations, both the foundation of our houses and of our home lives. We can't repair damage if we don't know about it. Paying attention and responding quickly is the way to go. What may be "small stuff" can more easily be acknowledged, forgiven, and changed now, rather than allowing resentment to build up over time and cause more damage.

- **Evaluate honestly.** Whether earlier or later, we need to be honest about our part in our relationship problems. Where do we need to be more forgiving? Where do we need to change our resentment-provoking behaviors? As with home inspections, honest evaluation is the starting place for the home improvements we want and need to make.

- **No shortcuts!** Foundation damage is serious and requires serious repairs. In the case of family relationships, "sorry" won't be enough to prove you're remorseful and serious about change. If you sincerely want to save your family life, commit to change in your heart. Then follow through, not only with a meaningful apology, but with consistently changed behavior.

- **Get off the cycle of resentment.** That cycle isn't going anywhere but down, so stop resenting a family member because they resent you. Accept that they're not perfect. Apologize for your own failures. Your example may lead them to apologize. Tell them you're serious about doing your part in making real and lasting home improvements.

- **Choose change.** If you need to forgive, then forgive! If you need to stop resentment-provoking behaviors, then stop! Change is rarely easy and takes time and effort. You may even need your loved ones, friends, a counselor, or God to hold you accountable. But get busy changing.

- **Start small, go big!** Forgiveness takes practice. Start with the "small stuff." Request change, and if you can change, why not? Make life as pleasant as possible for each other. If they don't change, then accept their humanity and "don't sweat the small stuff." As you and your family embrace a forgiving attitude toward each in the small stuff, you'll strengthen that same forgiving attitude for the big stuff that needs forgiveness.

- **Risk being vulnerable.** Admitting that we have failed—that we've been unforgiving and/or hurtful— requires vulnerability, which can be scary. However, with effort, we can both admit and accept that we and our loved ones have failed and will fail again. That's the beginning of forgiveness and the beginning of freedom!

BIG REVEAL

The following story may help you envision the payoff for increasing forgiveness at home. Shannon shares, "A woman I once helped was honest about her feelings of resentment. Her husband had prioritized purchasing his 'toys,' as she called them, and in doing so, had withheld financial resources for things she wanted and needed. In turn, she resented him.

"I validated her feelings but challenged her to consider how her resentment was imprisoning her and pushing her husband further away emotionally. She got honest with herself and began softening her heart toward her husband. She admitted that her resentment had caused her to withdraw from him. To her husband's credit, he, too, was ready to make change. In time, and with counseling, they were able and willing to forgive each other for grudges they had been holding."

Whatever your plans for decreasing resentment and increasing forgiveness, start imagining now how freeing it will feel to forgive and be forgiven. Let that freedom be what propels you forward in your home improvement efforts!

TALK IT OVER

1. Think about a time that you failed but were able to forgive yourself and be forgiven by someone else. How can that experience help you now with forgiving yourself and your family?

2. Which of your family members' behaviors have contributed to your feelings of resentment? How have you expressed resentment toward them?

3. How have your loved ones expressed resentment toward you?

4. What next step are you willing to take to address your family's need for increasing forgiveness at home? Consider getting their thoughts on next steps, too.

HOME IMPROVEMENT GOAL:
Clear up confusion.

HOME IMPROVEMENT TOOL:
Improve communication.

Chapter 6

IMPROVING COMMUNICATION

Everything flows a lot easier through unclogged pipes.

#yougottalaugh

GARY: Marriage is a lifelong teacher and test of our communication skills. Skipping "classes" is not recommended!
#Communication 101: listen, then listen some more!

SHANNON: What's a communication expert's favorite Christmas song? You guessed it: "Do You Hear What I Hear?"
#Communication breakdowns aren't always the other person's fault.

WE CAN HAVE beautiful sinks and faucets, but if our pipes are clogged or leaky, we've got problems. Best-case scenario, we've got annoying backups or dripping sounds; worst-case scenario, we've got corrosion or water damage.

Because communication is similar to the pipes in our homes, when I talk with couples and families about home improvement, I ask, "Are your lines of communication clear, clogged, or leaky?"

Clear lines of communication are those in which people avoid confusion by listening to understand and responding in supportive ways, especially in tense situations. Anyone can listen and be positive in easy situations, but the tense situations are the truer test of our communication skills and commitment to supportive, relationship-building communication.

Clogged lines of communication are those in which we're not effectively expressing ourselves or listening to others, which leads to confusion between us. Here are some common culprits of clogged communication: distracted listening, insensitive responses, disrespectful words, poor timing, harsh tone, bad attitude, the silent treatment or cold shoulder, "stuck record" syndrome, and vague or too little information.

Leaky lines of communication are those in which we confuse others by expressing ourselves with too much detail, too much "drama," or too much "all about me" talk. Problematic as these common culprits of leaky lines can be, they can simply be part of a person's personality or their age and stage in life and, as such, may require acceptance and patience on the part of family members.

Lack of emotional support is another common cause of leaky lines of communication. Sometimes one or more family members have unmet emotional needs and, in response, are overflowing, or "leaking" hurt emotions in the form of unproductive confrontation, tearfulness, angry outbursts, or grudge-holding. The hurt feelings behind the "leakiness" are often valid and warrant attention, just as the leaky pipes in our houses need attention. Yet, as clearly as we think we're expressing ourselves, or as clearly as we think we're understanding the other person, we are talking and listening through leaky lines of communication. The result: misunderstanding and more hurt feelings.

People with clear lines of communication occasionally work with counselors to improve their already good communication. More often, it's people's clogged or leaky lines of communication that bring them to counseling. Unfortunately, they've sometimes waited so long to get help that their communication has either grown increasingly negative or has shut down altogether.

IS THIS YOU?

Are you thinking about your family's communication problems? Perhaps you can relate to the following examples of communication problems Shannon and I frequently hear in counseling:

"Sometimes it feels like we speak two different languages. She says, 'How could you say such a thing to me?' I say, 'What do you mean? That's not what I meant at all.'"

"My parents just don't understand. I can't talk to them."

"I wish my teenager would talk with me. Instead, I just get eye rolls and shoulder shrugs."

"I thought you meant . . ."

"How many times do I have to tell you to . . . ?"

"I get so tired of repeating myself."

"Funny, I get tired of you repeating yourself, too."

"I couldn't remember all the things you told me to do, so I just did the ones I could remember."

"Her family is loud and opinionated. The first time I went to Thanksgiving with them, I was way out of my comfort zone."

"His family is quiet, but I know they're talking behind the scenes. I'd rather they just tell me what they're thinking."

"You constantly interrupt me."

"Her silence speaks volumes. There have been times when she has gone two whole days without speaking to me."

"He holds grudges and brings up old stuff all the time."

"You're always so angry. I don't know what you want from me."

These and other types of communication problems evoke a spectrum of emotions for family members, among them, frustration, anger, sadness, and hopelessness. Important as these emotions are, they often result from confusion that is caused by clogged and leaky lines of communication. To decrease confusion, couples and families need the essential home improvement tool of clear lines of communication.

WHY IS TALKING AND LISTENING SO HARD?

Why is communication so important? Because none of us are mind readers! If we are going to process life as a team, then I must be willing to share with you some of what I am thinking and feeling, and you must be willing to listen. Then you reveal your thoughts and feelings while I listen. Talking and listening: Why is that so difficult? Because we have not been trained to listen.

It has been said that the average person will listen for seventeen seconds before they interrupt and give their idea. We listen to respond, rather than listening to understand what the other person is thinking and feeling. Until we understand their thoughts and feelings, our response will likely miss the mark, and thus be unproductive or even destructive.

When your spouse or child is speaking, imagine that you have elephant ears. You are concentrating on listening, not planning your response. Ask questions to make sure you understand what they are saying and feeling. "Are you saying that you feel disappointed because I failed to . . ." They may answer, "Disappointed, yes, but also angry because I think you treated me unfairly."

How do you respond? First, affirm their feelings. "I guess I can see why you would feel angry. Now, let me give you my perspective." Since you heard them express their "side," they will likely listen to you.

We aren't always going to say the perfect thing at the perfect time.

But for all of us, part of the problem with clearing our clogged and leaky lines of communication is that we put so much pressure on ourselves and others to get it just right that we end up hurting rather than helping our communication. So what can we do to keep our expectations reasonable when trying to decrease confusion and increase communication at home?

For starters, we accept that we all are human. Thus, we aren't always going to say the perfect thing at the perfect time. We are going to misunderstand, misjudge, and miss opportunities to be loving and supportive. And, yes, we are going to overreact in stressful moments, and that's not only true of your toddler or your teenager, but of you as well.

As someone once said, "I've learned that people will forget what you said, people will forget what you did, but people will never forget how you made them feel."[1]

We will miss the mark with our communication at times, but we don't have to miss the mark with the "heart" behind our communication. Do we love our loved ones enough that we will listen and speak to each other with respect, kindness, patience, and love—even in hard times? Will we quickly apologize and ask for forgiveness upon realizing or being told we blew it with our words, tone, eye rolls, shoulder shrugs, silent treatment, or angry rants? And will we commit to continually improve in our communication efforts?

DRAWING UP THE PLANS

So where do we go from here? As your home improvement consultants, Shannon and I want to share with you our "High 5" communication model.

High 5 consists of five Cs: considerate, calm, clear, concise, and consistent. These each have a very simple and practical application for improving communication at home.

Considerate. In chapter 1, we talked about consideration as a home improvement tool for decreasing selfishness. That's true here, too. To increase communication with our loved ones, we need to *consider* not only our thoughts and feelings but theirs as well. Begin by asking yourself what's going on in you that you're not listening, not expressing yourself in positive ways, or not responding to your loved ones in positive ways. Even children can learn to answer the question, "Why do you think you spoke harshly to your mother?" "Do you think you need to apologize?" Reflection on our negative responses helps us to be more considerate in the future.

Calm. How often do we blow it with our loved ones by not controlling our temper? For most of us, the answer is "a lot." And that doesn't help with improving understanding and encouragement in our relationships. People will say, "But I am calm!" Or, "How can I *not* be mad?" Right . . . your "calm" and my "calm" may be two different things. And yes, we sometimes need to express disappointment or disapproval. But staying calm, or even more calm than normal, helps us communicate clearly without doing damage to our relationships.

> How often do we blow it with our loved ones by not controlling our temper? For most of us, the answer is, "a lot."

Clear. People sometimes say too much or too little. Listeners can get lost in the detail or need more detail to fully understand the speaker's intention. Or we become distracted, either by something around us or an emotional "distraction" such as unforgiven resentment toward the other person. Add potentially negative nonverbal communication such as eye rolls, shoulder shrugs, grimaces, sighs—and you've got a recipe for confusion on both sides! How do we solve this? We say less or we say more; we minimize distractions; we forgive (see chapter 5); we don't overreact to the other's nonverbal responses, and we monitor our own. Is all this easy? No! But these efforts will lead to clearer communication.

Concise. Less is more! Say a lot if you like, but people will remember the most important points. As the speaker, make sure your most important points are clear. As a listener, feel free to ask for clarification. "What is your most important point? I want to make sure I understand." Being concise is especially good for giving direction to children or giving direction in stressful circumstances. The clearer and more concise, the better!

Consistent. Circumstances change and require some flexibility in our responses. However, the more consistent we can be with our responses, the more our loved ones will expect and accept our response. If we say "I'll be home at 6:00" or "we will buy you something small at the store," then we need to strive to stick with what we said barring unexpected circumstances. Unexpected circumstances require our loved ones to themselves exercise flexibility.

DO-IT-YOURSELF

High 5 is not just good for your spouse and family, it's good for you! Examining your own communication strengths and weaknesses and then working to improve those is a good way of leading by example in your family.

What are your communication strengths and weaknesses? How did you develop those strengths and minimize your weaknesses?

You might enlist your loved ones to help you identify what your communication strengths and weaknesses are. Ask them, "What do I do to show you that I'm listening?" "What is something you wish I did more of to show you that I care when you're talking to me?" "Is there something I do or say that gets on your nerves?"

Cali laughed when I suggested this approach. She said, "Bring it on! I'm always taking little communication surveys and thinking about stuff like this, so this should be fun. Of course, I've never really asked my family before, so I'm curious to hear what they'll say."

Just like Cali, you should approach this assignment neutrally; do not overreact if your family says something hurtful. Instead, tell them you're going to take their comments to heart and do some additional investigation. Include in your research some reflection on your childhood family life and previous relationships. Think about how those influenced your communication patterns. Celebrate the positive communication skills you picked up over time, but ask yourself why you've held on to any negative communication skills.

You'll also want to assess which of your spouse and kids' communication habits trigger either positive or negative responses in you. This type of assessment is a way of identifying positive and negative experiences of the past that affect our present reactions.

Thankfully, whatever your communication weaknesses are, that's not the end of the story. We all can and should continually "rewrite" our stories to improve on the old and incorporate new and improved communication habits. And that's how you do it yourself!

 ## ALL-IN BUDGET

Shannon talks about having "store wars" with her children. You as a parent or grandparent will relate. Store wars happen because children are children and don't always understand or accept that they can't have a toy every time they're in a store. Store wars also happen because, like Shannon, parents aren't always consistent with their yeses and nos. "I'd like to say my kids have beat me down over time or that they catch me in weak moments, but the truth is, they sometimes keep asking for toys because I've been inconsistent with my answer in the past. I'll say, 'You can't have a toy this time,' then end up changing my mind."

Shannon isn't unusual. Whether it's inconsistent messages or another issue, most of us need to improve our communication, and it takes everyone in the family to make it happen.

I recommend that families get *all* members *in*volved with increasing communication by practicing High 5. This will require some teaching on your part. You can teach High 5 in a number of creative ways, but one way would be to post all five communication tips on a poster or white board at home so that they're visible to the family. You might even make this a checklist of sorts so that any time a family member catches another family member being considerate, calm, clear, concise, or consistent, they could put a check or sticker on the board. Along with charting the family's progress, you can add more fun by literally high-fiving each other any time someone demonstrates one of the five Cs.

SWEAT EQUITY

You might have a slow drain in your house where the pipe has gotten narrowed over time. You learn to live with it because you don't want to deal with a plumber. But eventually . . . you might have to pick up the phone. So it is with clogged and leaky lines of communication. That may work if the lines aren't *too* clogged or too leaky, but after a while, you have to decide, "Do I want us to keep treating each other this way, or can we do better? Can we repair our communication so that it flows clear and easy between us?" The answer is yes, you and your family can and should get to work on clearing lines of communication. The sweat equity will pay off!

In chapter 6, we've explored the home improvement tool of communication. The following is a recap of important tips for clearing up confusion and improving communication:

- **Check your pipes!** Clogged and leaky pipes can happen before you realize it but also can be something you know about and allow to go on for far too long. Routine monitoring and thoughtful, attentive repair can not only clear the lines of communication between you and your loved ones but can prevent more damaging communication breakdowns.

- **Don't wait too long.** You may know firsthand the emotional pain that can happen when we as people wait too long to repair communication breakdowns. Perhaps you know because your parents didn't model healthy communication for you as a child, or maybe you know because of your own poor communication habits in previous relationships. Now is the time to tend to clogged and leaky lines of communication. Putting in the sweat equity now will save you some regret down the road.

- **Communication matters!** You and your loved ones want the same thing—to be understood and encouraged.

You and they can accomplish those mutual goals despite your different communication strengths and weaknesses. Rather than being frustrated, disappointed, or discouraged by your loved ones' clogged or leaky lines, help them, and let them help you as you and they work together to clear the lines of communication between you.

- **"Perfect" is impossible.** You and your loved ones won't always say the right thing at the right time. However, you and they will long remember how you treated one another. So instead of working toward "perfect" communication, listen as well as you can, speak kindly to each other, ask for clarification whenever you need it, apologize when you offend each other, and regularly remind each other that you genuinely want to understand and support each other.

- **Don't blame everybody else.** Yes, like you, your loved ones have some annoying and negative communication habits, and yes, those trigger some of your own bad habits. But we each have to take responsibility for our own poor communication. Work harder to correct your bad habits rather than focusing on those of others.

- **No more store wars!** We certainly can't blame our children for our clogged lines of communication. As we continue to improve our own communication habits, we'll see an improvement in their communication habits.

- **High 5!** Decide together as a family that you'll give each other as many High 5s as possible. Be as considerate, calm, clear, concise, and consistent in your communication with each other as possible. And yes, every time you do, why not give each other a high five to celebrate your success!

BIG REVEAL

Imagine you and your loved ones saying things like:

"Thank you for listening."

"Thank you for putting your phone down and looking at me when I talk to you."

"Thank you for asking me what I meant rather than assuming the worst."

"Thank you for valuing my opinion."

"Thank you for not turning everything into a joke."

"Thank you for your patience."

"Thank you for supporting me no matter what."

"Okay. Will do."

"I don't know what I'd do without you."

"I thank God for you!"

Don't these sound refreshing? These all represent amazing big-reveal types of moments for couples, parents, and children. They don't always come easily, but they're not as far off as you might think. You've got this!

TALK IT OVER

1. What signs of clogged or leaky communication lines have you seen in your family lately? What has been the result?

2. This week, note when one of your family has been considerate, calm, clear, concise, and/or consistent in their communication with you. Make a point of expressing your appreciation to them.

3. When lately have you been tempted to blame someone else for your clogged or leaky lines of communication? Have you apologized? When have you been blamed by someone else for their clogged or leaky lines? Have they apologized?

HOME IMPROVEMENT GOAL
Reduce control.

HOME IMPROVEMENT TOOL
Enhance trust.

Chapter 7

ENHANCING TRUST

We can control thermostats; we can't control people.

#yougottalaugh

GARY: Sooner or later, your children *will* leave the nest (they may later fly back). #Trust they know where you live!

SHANNON: Hello, my name is Shannon. I struggle daily with trying not to control everything and everyone around me. #Trust that life does go on just fine without you and me trying to over-control it.

ENERGY-EFFICIENT HEATING and cooling has been and will continue to be an important conversation in the home improvement world. Why? Because energy efficiency saves people money, which frees up funds for other important needs in life. Energy efficiency also conserves the world's energy resources, and this, too, is an important consideration.

Considering the importance of energy efficiency, we can't afford to overlook our heating and cooling systems when renovating our homes. We might be tempted to change only the things we see (walls, floors, appliances, amenities), but we won't be able to enjoy them as much if we're uncomfortable due to unresolved HVAC problems.

Like our homes, we as people have energy efficiency issues. Among our issues—we have "thermostat" problems. I'm talking about an emotional temperature. We can be hot one day and cold the next. We need more consistency so we are not constantly running back to the thermostat. Controlling our own internal "temperature" (mood, choices, etc.) is challenging enough, but we also try to control our loved ones' thoughts, feelings, and choices. Trying to control everything and everybody around us is not sustainable long-term and, thus, not energy efficient. We truly can waste a lot of precious energy, as well as damaging precious relationships over time, when we are overly controlling of our family.

When I talk with couples and families about control, we're usually talking about healthy versus unhealthy forms of control. For example, control has no place in a healthy adult relationship, and so if this is an issue for you and your spouse, you may need to seek out a "home improvement expert" (professional counselor) to help you improve in the area of feeling and expressing mutual respect. There is much more to say about control issues in marriage, but in this chapter, we have chosen to focus on challenges parents face with controlling and/or trusting their children. We have found that this is an issue most parents struggle with.

CONTROL: WHAT'S THE RIGHT BALANCE?

Control, however, is a realistic and necessary part of parenting because children need direction and correction. As they age and gain more life experience, they are better able and expected to take on more control and responsibility in decision-making. In turn, we as parents can gradually exert less control.

This all sounds great, and, in fact, many of us as parents agree. We say, "Yes, children need age-appropriate opportunities to make decisions for themselves. In doing this, they will learn that all decisions have consequences. Thus they will learn and be better prepared for adulthood."

But as parents, we know it isn't easy to find the right balance of control and letting go, just like it isn't always easy to find a temperature on our thermostat that's "just right." Sometimes, as parents, we exert more or less control than we should. We may do things for children that they should do for themselves, or on the flip side, we may give children more responsibility than they developmentally are capable of handling.

Finding the right balance between too much and too little control takes a lot of energy. Do we tie our child's shoes for him or give him time to do it himself? Do we limit screen time or trust our child to monitor herself? What happens if we're running late for school or church, and our kid is still struggling over his shoelaces? Do we jump in? Or what if we give our daughter more freedom to determine her screen time, and we find her texting when she's supposed to be doing homework?

You may say, "Get the kid flip-flops or slide-ons," or "Eliminate the argument—thirty minutes of screen time per day is enough." And yes, parents have to decide for themselves how they'll handle the day-to-day challenges of parenting. But in my experience, parental decision-making is not always so easy or clear-cut. Your son says, "I don't want to tie my shoes, and the other shoes don't stay on when we go to the playground." Your daughter argues, "My friends' parents let them have a Facebook account. Why can't I?"

Shoes and devices are among some of the easier decisions we make as parents. How much more complicated does the matter of too much or too little control become when we start talking about curfews, money management, and sexual relationships?

To be energy-efficient with control, you'll need the home improvement tool of trust—trust in your children's ever-developing capabilities and trust in each other that you, together, can figure out the best balance of control between you. Wise use of the tool of trust will lead to a decrease in control-related problems at home, which means energy savings for you and your family!

THE TOOL OF TRUST

It's a good feeling to know that people trust you! That's the same good feeling your children feel when you allow them age-appropriate opportunities to take initiative and make decisions. When we do for them what they can do for themselves, we not only expend more energy than we need to, but we also send them the message, "you're weak." By trusting your children, you send the opposite message: "I believe in you. I believe you can do this!"

Developmental psychologist Dr. Erik Erikson recognized the importance of children having developmentally appropriate opportunities to grow their capabilities. In his psychosocial stages of development model, the first four of the eight stages relate to trust.[1] Stage 1, in fact, is a time wherein children develop either trust or mistrust in their parents' dependability. In stage 2, which occurs between eighteen months and age three, children either feel confident enough to exercise autonomy, or they feel self-doubt. Then in stage 3, children ages three to five feel either that they are free to exert initiative or that they will be made to feel guilty if they take too much initiative. And in stage 4, children ages five through twelve either feel competent to accomplish their goals, or they feel inferior and incapable of accomplishing their goals.

Parents play an essential role in helping children successfully develop trust, autonomy, initiative, and competence during these foundational stages of life. We succeed in our role as parents by believing enough in their capabilities that we allow them age-appropriate challenges and support them as they fail and succeed. They won't develop to their fullest capacity if we exercise more than necessary control and prevent them from healthy opportunities for decision-making.

Another reason that it's important for parents to convey trust in our children is that, if we don't, they will misbehave. Think about that! If we trust our children, we can reduce their misbehavior. That was psychiatrist Dr. Rudolf Dreikurs's theory[2] anyway, and one that I agree with. Building on psychologist Dr. Alfred Adler's work, Dreikurs said that behind children's misbehavior is their need for power, attention, revenge, or encouragement. Viewing misbehavior in this way helps us as parents respond to our children's misbehavior much differently than we typically might. Perhaps instead of us having all the power, they need us to allow them age-appropriate power. Or perhaps they need our encouragement as they work through a challenge as opposed to us handling the challenge for them.

A final reason for increasing trust is that trusting our children is not only good for them; it's good for us. For one, we don't have enough energy to consistently control our children's every move, and so allowing them appropriate freedom helps us sustain our energy. Second, because we one day will want them to be prepared for adulthood, we need to be willing now to allow them to practice self-control. And third, we need help! Allowing and expecting our children to take initiative gives us extra hands and help around the house. That's a win-win. Kids get hands-on life practice, and parents get helpers when it comes to picking up toys, clearing the table, folding clothes, walking the dog, mowing the grass, and much more!

DRAWING UP THE PLANS

Fundamentally, control has to do with decision-making. As parents, we want our children to learn to make wise decisions. How will they learn if we make all the decisions for them?

In the younger years, one of the best approaches is to let the child make choices between options the parent offers. For example, "Would you like to put your bike in the garage before dinner or after dinner?" The child has a choice. If they fail to follow through and leave the bike outside, they lose bike privileges for a day.

Another example relates to television. Parents choose a few programs that they deem appropriate for their child's age. Then say, "Here are three programs that you may choose from, but you can only watch television for thirty minutes each day. You can choose which one you want to watch." Giving the child choices within boundaries is communicating trust and gives the child the responsibility of decision-making. Choosing between options is a skill they will need later as adults.

Like the subject of energy efficiency, the subject of parenting has received a lot of attention in recent years. Among some of the more talked-about parenting concepts have been helicopter parents, free-range parents, Velcro parents, and tiger moms.

Helicopter parents hover, ready to rescue their children at a moment's notice from social and emotional distress.[3] Free-range parents allow their children to take safe risks with minimal parental supervision.[4] Velcro parents "stick to" their children, allowing little independence and protectively filtering much that their children see and do.[5] Tiger moms are strict and demand high-level achievement by their children.[6]

These parenting approaches aren't necessarily "bad" or "wrong." In fact, generally speaking, helicopter parents, free-range parents, Velcro parents, and tiger moms are loving, devoted parents who want the best for their children. Yet each approach has its downsides.

But for all parents, the question is, how much do you trust that your children are capable and ready to take on various responsibilities? The more capable and ready, the more control you can comfortably turn over to your children.

You and your kids will need lots of practice to pull off the home life improvement of increased trust. This much-needed renovation won't happen overnight.

DO-IT-YOURSELF

Before expecting your family to change, what control-related changes do *you* need to make? Do you tend to lean toward over-controlling or under-controlling, or are you fairly balanced (energy-efficient) already?

Philosopher Dr. Dallas Willard said, "When you've done this [rested] enough to convince yourself that the world will be able to function without you, you will find true rest."[7] This is a humbling truth for people who tend to be over-controlling. A parent may say, "But my child needs me, and honestly, I don't look forward to the time when they don't need me as much." Yes, this is a loving, relationally connected, and healthy way of thinking about our role as parents. Yet ultimately, our children don't need to be so dependent on us that we or they think they can't go on without us.

Children do need their parents! Parents are important influencers and supporters of children. We're best able to maximize our influence and support when we're energy-efficient and are neither over- nor under-controlling of our children. The sweet spot between the two provide the right balance of control such that we can direct and correct and our children can strive and thrive.

You may or may not intend to be over- or under-controlling. You may be a go-with-the-flow kind of parent whose choices depend on the situation. My encouragement to you is to recognize where you're sometimes unintentionally being over- or under-controlling for the sake of convenience.

"I do that," admits Shannon. "I really want to give my kids healthy opportunities at self-control, but if we're in a hurry or stressed out, I'll sometimes tell them what to do and leave them little to no choice in the matter. Or out of frustration, I may just give in totally and allow them to have all the power."

Like Shannon, you may fluctuate at times. None of us are perfect! But you can and should continue to lead your family in energy efficiency by doing it yourself—finding the right balance between healthy and unhealthy control every chance possible.

ALL-IN BUDGET

Control, by its nature, sometimes involves a battle. We fight each other because we don't trust that things will work out in our favor if the other person has more control than we do. And sometimes our fears are well founded. This is where trust comes in.

To make lasting home improvement, the whole family will need to steadily work toward building trust in each other. Parents will need to trust their children with more age-appropriate opportunities for self-control; children will need to trust that their parents have their best interests at heart when they allow or limit various freedoms. This, of course, is easier said than done, but the bigger the issue, the more important it will be for parents, in particular, to stick to their blueprint for change.

One family I helped had a fourteen-year-old son and nineteen-year-old daughter. The parents had previously allowed both of them privileges and rewarded them for responsible behavior. At one point, though, the son began to push the envelope by sneaking behind his parents' backs to listen to music and watch television programs that were not approved. They reiterated their concerns about inappropriate content but agreed to allow him a little more freedom. Any time his parents "caught" him being responsible, they praised him. Any time they caught him abusing his freedom, he lost his devices for extended periods of time.

As for the daughter, when she came home from college for visits, she stayed out late without notifying her parents of her plans. What's a parent to do? Curfews with young adult children require more flexibility than previously. Yet the daughter owed her parents the respect of honoring their home and expectations. When they threatened to discontinue her financial support, she began exerting more—but not full—self-control. Her ongoing irresponsibility over the next year finally led to her parents appropriately exerting self-control for themselves—they didn't want to "kick her out" but instead assisted her with planning a budget and getting a job and then leasing her own apartment.

See what I mean about "fight"? Control-related problems aren't always easy. Your best bet as a parent is to be consistent with the message: "We might not always agree, but we're in this together, and we are always going to do what we believe is best for you." Remind your children often that **all** of you have to be **all in** when it comes to control. You can provide healthy opportunities for self-control, but your kids, too, need to step up efforts at rewarding your trust in them with responsible self-control.

 ## SWEAT EQUITY

As with literal home improvement, families have to invest a lot of thought, time, and energy into improving relationships and home life. This is all the more reason we need to be energy-efficient when it comes to dealing with control-related problems. We need to save energy every chance we can so that we have energy for all the other work that needs to be done!

In chapter 7, we've explored the home improvement tool of trust. The following is a recap of important tips for decreasing control-related problems and increasing trust:

- **Give up.** You can't control everything and everybody. It's just not possible! Giving up that unrealistic goal will be more freeing than you realize. You'll waste less energy, and your loved ones can use more of their own energy to figure out their own challenges. That's good for you and for them!

- **Give in.** Sometimes we don't want to give other people control because we don't want to give in to their way of thinking and doing things. Trust me: unless it's a life-and-death matter, it's okay to give in to other people's healthy desires and need for control. You may be encouraged to see that they are surprisingly capable!

- **Get moving!** Now's the time to prepare your children for adulthood. We'd like to think that we have a long time before they have to fly our nests, but we don't have as much time as we think. Tying shoes, washing dishes, making beds, vacuuming, taking out the trash, doing the bulk of school projects on their own, working a job a few hours a week, managing a checking account . . . these are important rites of passage. Children may balk at times and may not want to pick up the control you're giving up, but it's good for them. They'll be better ready to launch when it comes time to fly the nest.

- **Get ready.** Control-related problems sometimes involve a "fight"—a battle for who is going to have more control, you or your child. While it may feel like a fight, we don't and shouldn't see these problems as a battle. Instead, we and our children fare better when we see these struggles as expected, healthy growing pains. Parents are growing accustomed to allowing their children healthy, age-appropriate opportunities for self-control; children are growing accustomed to taking on more responsibility. In this way of thinking, control-related problems are more purposeful than painful. Share this perspective with your children so that they know where you're coming from when working through control issues.

- **Trust is a must.** Yes, we as people need to earn the trust of others, but we as parents have to give our children opportunities to earn trust. Then we have to accept that mistakes and failure are okay and part of how our children will learn and grow. We can direct and correct our children; that's an important part of parenting and of childhood. But we shouldn't hold mistakes and failures against them. Rather, we need to trust them with lots of chances at practicing self-control—taking initiative, making decisions, correcting mistakes, figuring out solutions to the challenges they face.

- **Trust your spouse.** I intentionally didn't focus this chapter on control and trust between spouses. Spouses cannot and should not try to control one another. If you and your spouse are trying to micro-manage or dominate one another, it's time for serious communication. If you can't solve it, then call for the help of a counselor or pastor. Controlling spouses are destroying their own marriages. In a healthy marriage, you must view each other as capable people with the right and the freedom to think and feel the way you want without the other person devaluing you or fighting you for control. If one or both of you has damaged the other person's trust, get serious about rebuilding trust. Trust is restored when you demonstrate that you are trustworthy. This will take time, but it is essential to marital health.

 ## BIG REVEAL

Driver's licenses, diplomas, first paychecks, and first homes represent significant "big reveal" moments. They prove that parents successfully gave and children successfully took control so that the children were ready when it came time to graduate from childhood into adulthood.

You don't have to wait for those milestone "big reveal" moments to enjoy the satisfaction of allowing your children healthy, age-appropriate opportunities for self-control. You likely have multiple opportunities every day to trust your children to make decisions, take initiative, and otherwise take responsibility for their choices. For example, depending on their age, they can pick out their own outfit, remember to bring their book bag, help wash dishes, end an unhealthy friendship by their own choosing, and fill the car up with gas without being asked.

Look for and celebrate these smaller "big reveal" moments as well. Ultimately, it will be these seemingly small, easily overlooked moments that lead to your increasing trust in your children's ability to handle responsibility and their increasing trust in themselves to be able to tackle life's challenges. That's energy efficiency at its best—you and your children continually finding and accepting a reasonable, effective balance of power!

TALK IT OVER

1. What makes it hard for you to give your children healthy, age-appropriate opportunities to practice self-control? What makes it easy?

2. When have you trusted your children with too much control too soon?

3. What have been some of your and your children's biggest battles related to control?

4. What rewards and consequences have you established for those occasions when your children do and do not behave responsibly?

HOME IMPROVEMENT GOAL:
Decrease shaming and blaming.

HOME IMPROVEMENT TOOL:
Develop compassion.

Chapter 8

DEVELOPING COMPASSION

The light of compassion is a light families can afford to leave on all the time!

> ### #yougottalaugh

GARY: Paying a service to do the hard work of window washing is a gift that keeps on giving! #Compassionate family members don't judge you for not liking to clean windows.

SHANNON: I want most every light in the house on; Stephen does not. I know he really loves me because he leaves the lights on for me. #Compassion says, "Lights are cheaper than counseling."

"IT'S JUST A STUPID TOY. Don't be such a baby!"

"Can't you get anything right?"

"Keep that up, and you'll never make the team."

"Be a man!"

"Maybe if you would've worked harder, you might have gotten that promotion."

"You've really let yourself go."

"What's with all the crying?"

"It's all your fault."

Do you hear the shame and blame in these comments? We would like to think families don't say these things to each other, but we do. Sometimes we're trying to be hurtful. That is, we consciously or subconsciously believe such words will somehow cause our loved ones to snap out of it, pull it together, or otherwise "just stop" any thoughts, feelings, and behaviors that we don't agree with or can't handle at that moment. Other times, we're not so much trying to be hurtful but are simply being thoughtless about the heartbreak our loved ones are experiencing.

What if couples and families became way more serious about seeing each other's hurt through a compassionate light? What if we lifted each other up instead of putting each other further down?

"I know that toy is important to you. Maybe we can fix it."

"We'll keep working on it. I'll help you."

"What do you need to do differently to make the team?"

"It's okay to be scared."

"I'm sorry you didn't get your promotion. You've worked so hard."

"You'll always look good to me! I love you inside and out."

"It's easy to see this thing has gotten you really down."

"It's not all your fault. I could have done more to help."

THE NEW LIGHT OF COMPASSION

Our responses change when we look at and think about our loved ones with compassion. Rather than rush to criticize, we patiently and gently sympathize. And beyond sympathy, we can often empathize with our spouse and children whenever we stop to realize that their struggles are like our own. After all, we know what it's like to hurt—to have a prized possession destroyed, to mess up, to feel the pressure of competition, to be overwhelmed with fear, to miss out on a raise or promotion, to struggle with much-needed personal changes, to feel down, and to feel responsible for failure.

Identifying with our loved ones in these ways can and should lead us to respond more compassionately to one another. For example, our "what's wrong with you" types of responses should become "I understand" types of responses. This more compassionate mindset helps us to clearly see our loved ones' hurts in a new light, which is an important home life improvement.

New lighting is also an important part of literal home improvement. Sometimes new light comes by way of simply cleaning our existing windows. Other times, we add windows where there were previously none. Why? Because windows allow in the beautiful and functional light of the sun and moon.

In addition to the light of the sun and moon, our homes are changed for the better with new and improved light fixtures. This is a simple and often affordable improvement that renovators and interior decorators make to modernize and add value to a home. More importantly, with improved and increased lighting, we as couples and families literally can see each other better and carry out our daily activities more effectively.

Compassion works the same as light. With more compassion, we see each other's struggles differently. Instead of seeing each other's hurts "dimly," as if through poor "lighting," we see each other in a more honest way. We recognize the hurt our loved ones feel, and rather than respond in harsh ways that only heap on more hurt, we can now choose to respond calmly and with sympathy and empathy. Ultimately, this is a much more encouraging way of supporting our spouse and children. Being hurtful toward one another, whether intentional or not, doesn't help anyone and, instead, creates emotional distance and bitterness.

If you and your family want to decrease hurtful responses, then get your home life toolbox ready for the tool of compassion. I believe you'll see each other in a whole new light thanks to this tool!

"I CARE ABOUT YOUR FEELINGS"

We know light is good for our physical and mental health. Like light, research also shows that compassion has many benefits. Researchers at Stanford University School of Medicine have scientifically proven that among compassion's benefits are pleasure, decreased levels of stress, and the strengthening of our immune system. Additionally, those researchers have found that compassion gives meaning to our lives.[1]

You may think of compassion as only something you show to the powerless and needy. You know—you give a few dollars to the homeless man on the corner, a new coat to the woman at the shelter, or Christmas gifts to the child in the local foster care system. Giving to and supporting others in this way is wonderful, and we each should do as much as we can to help those who are less fortunate. But I'm challenging you to see yourself and your loved ones as people in need of compassion. You may or may not have all the health and wealth you need, but more than this, you and your spouse and children daily experience the hardships of being human—you all feel the pain of failure and loss of one kind or another. As a family, some of the greatest gifts you give to each other is understanding and support. That's compassion! Without it, you're in essence saying, "Good luck. You're on your own!" With it, your message is much different: "I know you're struggling. I care about your feelings. I've got your back!"

Shannon and I often help couples and families who are working on being more compassionate with each other. A common scenario is one in which one or both spouses grew up in homes where they weren't shown compassion. They haven't had healthy models for giving or receiving compassion.

One husband told me, "My dad was a 'never-let-them-see-you-cry' kind of guy. If

> You may think of compassion as something you only show to the powerless and needy.

I showed emotion, he called me names and made fun of me. So now, if I see my wife or children struggling, I find myself telling them to 'stop crying' or to 'get over it.'"

A wife said, "I wish I could share my struggles with my husband, but I feel like he will think less of me. I don't know how to open up to him like he says he wants me to."

In contrast, Shannon shares a story of grandparents who, in the absence of their grandchildren's parents, raised the children and, from early on, encouraged them to talk openly about their struggles. "These were older people who were already digging deep energy-wise to raise their grandchildren. On top of providing the basics of life, they were compassionate toward the children's feelings of loss and wanted them to feel free to talk to them or their counselor any time they needed to."

Shannon told me of another family she worked with, a family whose child had special needs. She said, "The parents were honest with each other and with others in their community about their struggles, and in doing so, they helped to educate and encourage people to see their son for his strengths and not just his limitations. They were compassionate toward themselves and their son, and they allowed others to be compassionate toward them."

As humans, we want and need compassion from the people around us. Hearing someone say, "It's okay to struggle" or "Thank you for opening up to me" are often breakthrough kinds of moments in which a person feels increased self-worth and renewed hope. Shannon and I have heard so many people over time express such feelings: "He didn't make me feel judged or ashamed." "Her encouragement meant more to me than she'll ever know." "I don't know where I'd be today without my family's belief in me." "Our community rallying around us made all the difference." These kinds of comments reflect the value and impact of receiving compassion.

Of course, giving compassion is equally valuable. Giving compassion helps us feel connected to those around us. It also helps us to "give back" or "pay forward" the compassion that we ourselves have benefited from in life. Compassion truly helps both the receiver and the giver.

 ## DRAWING UP THE PLANS

The dirtiest windows and dimmest rooms would seem to be the ideal places to start when improving the lighting in a house. What about compassion? Where do we start to build that in our family?

We need to start at the top, so let's first assess compassion between you and your spouse. Are you as compassionate with each other as you would like to be?

"Stephen and I have a strong relationship, but I know I am not always compassionate enough toward him," Shannon shares. "When you're busy and tired, it's hard to be sensitive to other people's needs. I have to remind myself to listen, to try to understand where he's coming from, and to not give pat answers or unwanted solutions."

Stephen doesn't need halfhearted listening or forced

> **Are you and your spouse as compassionate with each other as you would like to be?**

sympathy; he, like all spouses, wants and needs to feel that Shannon is *for* him . . . that she genuinely cares about his thoughts and feelings. That's how we as couples draw closer together.

Karolyn and I have found that, after fifty years of marriage, we still have to make a concerted effort to see each other through a compassionate light. We're human, and so it's easy to get caught up in our own needs and be less kind and supportive toward each other than we'd like. One way we work to stay in sync with each other is by having a daily "sharing time." We share openly with each other about what's going on in our lives, we validate each other's feelings, and we ask one another what we can do to help.

Make time for each other. Talk. Listen. Validate each other's feelings. And ask how we can help. These are my recommendations to you and your family. Some couples and parents will say, "That sounds great, but we don't do the whole talking-listening thing so well. Besides, we're all doing our own thing anyway."

That's a big part of the problem—couples and families are doing their own thing and not making time to consider each other's thoughts and feelings. If you're skeptical about being able to allow thirty minutes each day, you can always start with ten minutes and work your way up. You and your family may be pleasantly surprised that you and they actually have more to share than you realized.

As couples and families talk and listen more, they can

then encounter another challenge. "What do I say in tough moments? What if I say the wrong thing?" If you're genuinely trying to be kind and supportive toward one another, your good intentions will shine through. Plus, if you mess up, you can model two more important home life improvement tools—the tool of apology and the tool of the do-over (a.k.a. "let me try that again").

Back to your plan. In what ways are you and your family struggling right now? In what ways are you and they either heaping on more hurt with hurtful reactions and responses or heaping on healing with compassionate reactions and responses?

 ## DO-IT-YOURSELF

Sometimes, people don't clean their windows, add new windows, or change their lighting because they're either not paying attention to how dimly lit their homes are, or maybe they don't want the benefits of improved lighting. Similarly, people aren't always paying attention to the effects of hurtfulness in their family life, or maybe they see the effects but feel powerless to make change.

Mahatma Gandhi said, "If we could change ourselves, the tendencies in the world would also change."[2] This same wisdom is true for us at home. We can be the change we wish to see in our homes. In this case, achieving increased compassion must begin with us.

As a starting point, are you compassionate toward yourself? That is, are you kind, encouraging, forgiving toward yourself? If not, I recommend that you "turn on the lights" inside yourself. Show yourself much-deserved compassion by accepting that you're imperfect. Allow yourself to make mistakes without reacting and responding harshly. Replace hurtful self-talk with positive talk: "I missed the mark this time; I'll keep trying." Validate your hurt feelings: "This would be hard for anyone. It's hard, and I'm going to allow myself time to recover."

Next, how compassionate are you toward others in your family? Are you kind, encouraging, forgiving of your spouse and children? Think back to how you've responded to them in recent days. Was your response calm and supportive? Or was your response harsh and hurtful? How might you change your responses going forward?

Honest self-reflection is an important do-it-yourself job, one that reminds me of how we need to clean both sides of a window to get a truly clear view. In the case of building compassion, we can't only look inward; we also have to look outward.

As Alex shared with me, "I'm trying to lighten up on myself and my children a bit mainly because I'm more and more hearing them beat themselves up for mistakes they make. After a lifetime of doing that to myself, I know firsthand that beating yourself up is simply adding hurt on hurt. You know, you feel bad about something and then put yourself down, and it's just a never-ending cycle."

With clear understanding of and commitment to your

family's need for compassion, you're now ready to model compassion for your family. Again, this means both showing compassion and asking for compassion from them. The more compassionate you are to each other, the more willing you'll each be to trust each other with your hurt feelings. One person's "light," or openness to another's hurt, invites the other's "light," or openness to sharing their hurt. Talk about benefits! What are you waiting for? It's time to do it yourself!

ALL-IN BUDGET

You're not alone if, when growing up, your parents said things like, "Who left the lights on?" or "Don't you know, lights cost money?" Now as a payer of bills, you maybe even say things like this yourself!

The good news about the light of compassion is that it's a light families can afford to leave on all the time. Being compassionate doesn't cost us anything— not really. You could say, "Compassion costs us energy." And you're right about that. But if we're going to expend energy on our families at all—and we will—why not pour that energy into compassion? Certainly it's a far better choice with far better outcomes than being hurtful toward each other.

> If we're going to expend energy on our families, why not pour that energy into compassion?

You're still reading, so I'm guessing you're *all in*. Now, you need some more ideas for getting your family to go *all in* with you.

I recommend that you invite your family to "leave the light on." You'll first have to explain how compassion is like the light in our homes—light improves our literal vision; compassion improves our emotional vision. With increased compassion, we're better able and more willing to see and respond to each other's emotional hurts with more kindness and sensitivity. You'll also need to explain that a compassionate family is one that is willing to share their emotional pain more openly because they trust that their loved ones genuinely care and want to encourage them when they're feeling down.

To make this "leave the light on" approach to building compassionate relationships even more interactive, invite your loved ones to say, "I need you to leave the light on for me" when they either need a family member's support or want to show support to a family member. Remember, compassion goes both ways—we need to ask to receive compassion at times, and at other times, we need to ask permission to show compassion, especially in instances where a loved one may be reluctant to share their emotional pain with us.

You and your family can also say, "Thank you for leaving the light on" when you notice another family member being compassionate. It may be that they're immediately kind and supportive toward another family member, or it could be that you see them ask for a do-over after being hurtful to a family member.

Either way, it's a positive effort and deserves celebration. The more you and your family "catch each other" being compassionate, the more likely you and they are to continue using this home life improvement tool.

SWEAT EQUITY

Home life improvement is as tiring in its own unique ways as literal home improvement. When it comes to increasing compassion, you and your family will be learning to shine the light of compassion inwardly and outwardly. You'll also be practicing asking for compassion when you need it and asking others to share their hurts with you so that you can be compassionate toward them. This is not natural for most of us. By nature, we are self-centered. We're also at a disadvantage if we grew up in homes where we didn't have good models of compassion. So how do we push through these challenges? We put in the sweat equity needed to achieve the compassionate home life we're in search of!

In chapter 8, we've explored the home improvement tool of compassion. The following recaps important tips for decreasing hurtfulness by increasing compassion:

- **Get serious!** Being kind and sensitive to others isn't always automatic. For one, we're human and, as such, tend to focus on our own needs more than other people's needs. Second, we're sometimes busy and tired and may either intentionally or unintentionally be thoughtless and insensitive when it comes to our loved ones' emotional pain. But if we are aware of a tendency toward inadvertent thoughtlessness, we can become more intentional, more serious, about treating our loved ones with compassion. In doing so, we become more supportive of those we care about the most rather than adding to their hurt with our dismissive and damaging words.

- **Check your responses.** Do you respond to your loved ones' emotional pain with calm, supportive words or with harsh, hurtful comments? Not sure? Ask your family. Or observe their reactions to your responses. Do they appear upset—or comforted? If upset, you likely can do more to express genuine concern for their feelings. You might start by remembering how you've been hurt in times past. Putting loved ones down or dismissing their feelings doesn't help heal their hurt; it makes them hurt worse. You know that from firsthand experience! Now is the time to choose to respond with more sympathy and empathy as a way of encouraging and supporting your loved ones through hard times.

- **Let there be light!** The sun and the moon are beautiful, functional sources of light. So, too, is improved, increased lighting in our homes. Compassion is another kind of light and one that helps us understand and respond in more sensitive ways to our loved ones when they're struggling. Through the light of compassion, we see each other more honestly than through the "dim light" of hurtfulness. Compassion brings healing; unkindness creates emotional distance and bitterness between us and our loved ones.

- **Compassion has its benefits.** You and I know from having given and received compassion the good feelings it brings. Scientific research further proves that, among other benefits, compassion gives meaning to life.[3] I would add that compassion brings meaning to our home life. Through our sensitivity and emotional support, we lift each other up, encourage self-worth, and help our loved ones build renewed hope that everything is going to work out okay. These are pretty amazing gifts when we're dealing with the many challenges of life.

- **Thirty minutes a day.** Couples and families sometimes miss opportunities to support one another because they simply don't make enough time together to connect. Find thirty minutes, or ten if thirty seems impossible, to talk, listen, validate each other's feelings, and ask how you can help each other. Making time to connect in this way keeps us informed of what's going on in each other's lives and allows us opportunity to show compassion to one another. You will need to tweak the amount of time and the language you use if you're talking with your younger children, but that shouldn't keep you from being compassionate toward them in ways they understand.

- **Leave the light on!** Emotional struggles can pop up at the least expected times. Encourage your family to be ready with compassion at any moment. Ask them to "leave the light on," the light of compassion, that is. Invite family members to reach out any time they feel they need emotional support (i.e., time, listening, validation, help), and ask if a family member will turn on "the light" of compassion for them. This may sound a little awkward at first, but little by little, you and your family's light of compassion will stay on. And that's a light you and they can afford to leave on!

BIG REVEAL

Imagine these big reveal possibilities . . .

Your four-year-old has a meltdown over losing her favorite doll. In less compassionate moments, you may have said, "You've got other dolls. What's so special about that one?" But with increased compassion, you choose to say, "Okay, we really don't have a lot of time to look, but where was the last place you had her?"

Your kids are fussing over who gets to watch what television program. In times past, they may have erupted into a shouting match, but this time, one of them says, "Who hasn't gotten to choose lately?" Then together they deliberate and decide who gets to choose.

You're stressed out and tired. You don't think anyone at home notices, but your spouse says, "I know you're tired, but I'd love to hear what's on your mind." That's a big change than in the past when you each might have just carried on in "survival mode" as opposed to reaching out to support each other.

Perhaps you're saying, "Yeah, that'll never happen for our family." And you're right—it won't happen if you and your family don't give your best effort at making good use of the home improvement tool of compassion. Give it a try! See what big reveal moments you and your family can accomplish together!

TALK IT OVER

1. What is your definition of compassion?

2. How well do you show yourself compassion?

3. When recently have you been compassionate toward your spouse or your kids? When did you respond in a hurtful way? How can you tell when you've hurt your spouse or children with your words?

4. How well do you ask for the compassion of others when you need it?

HOME IMPROVEMENT GOAL:
Control anger.

HOME IMPROVEMENT TOOL:
Increase patience.

Chapter 9

INCREASING PATIENCE

An open-door policy is only as inviting as the person on the other side of the open door.

> #yougottalaugh

GARY: My family has never been door slammers, unless, of course, you count loudly closing cabinet doors. Does that count? #Patience is welcome here!

SHANNON: Being patient requires a lot of energy. I sometimes have to take breaks. #Patience is literally someone's middle name, not mine, but someone's!

DOORS ARE A pretty important feature in our homes. They welcome us and our invited guests in, and they protect us from uninvited "guests."

Given the importance of doors, it's no wonder that door upgrades are on many people's home renovation wish lists. Fresh paint, new knobs and locks, or altogether new doors—these are just a few of the options when it comes to improving the character and functionality of doors.

We can also learn a lot from doors when it comes to the home improvement problem of anger. More specifically, in this chapter, we're talking about how we as couples and families literally and emotionally either shut each other out or invite each other in when we're angry. That is, we either push each other away and deal with our anger alone, or we work together to push through our anger in supportive, productive ways.

Despite frequent reminders not to, Shannon and Stephen's children shut and lock their bedroom doors when they are angry with one another. One time, this backfired in an unexpected way. Carson and Presley alerted their parents that Avery had locked his door and was stuck in his room, and sure enough, he was!

"Something in the doorknob broke so that Avery couldn't unlock the door from the inside, and we couldn't unlock it from the outside," Shannon said. "Stephen tried unsuccessfully to jimmy the door open. Finally, he had the great idea to slide a screwdriver under the door to Avery, who was then able to unscrew the doorknob from the door. With the knob removed completely, they could then open the door."

The Wardens' door troubles are a great illustration of the anger problems that so many couples and families experience. We get mad and need some emotional space, which is fine. However, we end up emotionally shutting each other out, when ultimately, our loved ones are the very ones we need to help us work through our anger.

Avery needed Presley to tell Shannon and Stephen that he was stuck in his room. They thought Avery wanted privacy and was being clever with his "locked in" excuse, and so they didn't respond quickly. Truly locked in his room, Avery next sent Carson to ask for help. Shannon investigated and confirmed that he was indeed stuck. She tried unsuccessfully to open the door and then called Stephen for help. After several attempts and lots of frustration, Stephen figured out how to help Avery unlock the door from the inside. Talk about teamwork!

After the lock-in episode, Stephen and Shannon processed the experience. They realized this was an example of what happens when we shut others out when we are angry. Avery was still in his room, feeling bad about the trouble he felt he had caused. So Stephen called him downstairs and explained, "No need to feel bad, Avery. That wasn't such a big waste of time after all! We all need to find a better way to handle anger. Rather than locking our doors, we need to leave our doors open so others can help us. "

LESS DESTRUCTIVE, MORE PRODUCTIVE

In addition to needing and allowing our loved ones to help us, we also learn how to manage our anger more effectively

> The emotion of anger is not wrong. However, we often do wrong things when we're angry.

when we take time to examine where our anger came from in the first place. Most of the time we get angry because in our mind someone treated us unfairly or spoke to us harshly. When we get angry with a family member this is almost always the case. The emotion of anger is not wrong. However, we often do sinful things when we are angry.

The problem is not anger, but how we respond to anger. If we don't exhibit patience, we can do some serious relationship damage when we are angry. In fact, in much the same way a demolition crew tears down a house, our angry words can quickly and completely demolish the love and trust we feel for one another. In more severe cases, destructive, unresolved anger can lead to divorce and tense co-parenting arrangements.

We have two kinds of anger: definitive and distorted. Definitive anger is what we feel when we encounter injustice. That is, somebody did somebody wrong. This kind of anger is a gift of God to motivate us to seek to right the wrong behavior. This calls for lovingly confronting the person who did wrong and hoping for an apology to which we respond with forgiveness. Distorted anger is what we feel when we don't get our way. What the person said or did was not morally wrong; it simply was not what we wanted them to say or do. Much of our anger in the family falls into this category. The husband is angry because his wife forgot to add his shirts to the laundry. Forgetting is not a sin. Forgetting is human. Three weeks later, the wife texts him and asks if he will stop by the store and get some milk. He agrees. When he arrives home, his wife is angry that he forgot the milk. In both cases, the anger is distorted anger. The answer lies not in lashing out with condemning words, but in looking for a way to get the milk home and the shirts to the cleaners. Then we can discuss what steps we might take to develop our memory in the future.

Whether definitive or distorted, we need to learn how to control anger rather than letting the anger control us. Our response needs to be productive rather than destructive. Where do you and your family fall on the destructive-productive continuum? Are you and they more destructive or more productive in handling anger?

Every family I know could improve their anger management with more patience toward each other. That's the home improvement tool that helps us, emotionally and relationally. With patience, we are more likely to leave the door open to meaningful communication rather than shutting the door and walking away in a rage.

A DOOR WITH A "WELCOME" SIGN

If someone is knocking at our door in an annoying or scary way, we're understandably not nearly as interested in letting them in as we are if they're knocking patiently and allowing us time to answer. If they are demanding that we open the door, we feel inclined to literally shut that person out.

Similarly, few people are going to come knocking on our door, or attempt to draw closer to us emotionally, if they know we feel hostile toward them. "They'll never get in here, and that's the way I like it!"

Our best chance of opening the literal and emotional doors between us when one or both of us is angry is if both people are patient. "I know you're angry. I'm willing to listen if you'll let me in." "I am angry, and yes please, come in. I'd love to be able to talk to you about what I'm thinking and feeling." This is really what we need in our most important relationships—the reassurance that, no matter what, we won't abandon each other. We're not only in it for "the better," but we're also in it for "the worse."

You could say patience is like a door with a "welcome" sign hanging on it, whereas anger is like a door with a "warning" sign hanging on it. The welcome sign conveys a message of "come on in"; the warning sign warns uninvited guests to proceed with caution. We each have to decide which sign we want to hang on the door. If we want healthy relationships, choosing the more patient, "welcome" approach is the way to go.

Karolyn and I have had lots of practice through the years with replacing our warning signs with welcome signs. We're peaceful people all in all, but we're still human, and humans get mad. In impatient moments, we've driven each other away in anger. But in patient moments, we've drawn close to each other for support. It didn't take us long to realize that patient was much better than impatient. Patience pulls us together; impatience only further contributes to anger and pushes us farther apart.

I've also counseled with countless other couples and families who've worked to decrease anger by increasing their patience with each other. Many have learned to productively push through anger together rather than push each other away in anger. But that's not always easy, and unfortunately, not every couple and family with whom I've worked were willing to become more patient. In some cases, the "angry one" let the anger control their behavior, rather than tempering anger with patience. In other cases, family members would not exercise patience toward the one who was angry. Without patience, these couples and families only added to their problems.

 ## DRAWING UP THE PLANS

Do you and your family have an open-door or closed-door policy when it comes to anger? That is, do you and your loved ones allow each other to be appropriately angry, and do you and they listen and encourage each other when working through anger? Or do you and your loved ones react negatively to anger and emotionally shut each other out rather than working together to productively push through anger?

I must confess that when we got married, I did not have a plan for handling anger. When we were "in love," I never anticipated that we would someday be angry with each other. I thought she was perfect and would always do what

I wanted. She thought the same about me. When we came down off the emotional euphoria of the "in love" high, we discovered our humanity. It took a while, but eventually we learned how to apply patience to our tool kit and process anger in a positive way. In this section, I want to share some simple ideas that I think will help you develop patience when you are angry or when you are responding to an angry spouse or child.

> When we came down off the emotional euphoria of the "in love" high, we discovered our humanity.

One: Give each family member the freedom to feel anger. It is a part of our humanity, and it cannot be eliminated. So help the family to understand that it is normal to feel anger.

Two: Teach them the two types of anger: definitive anger is when someone has done wrong toward another family member. Distorted anger is when we simply did not get our way.

Three: Don't blow up! That is, don't lash out with loud, harsh words, or actions that will hurt the other person. Such behavior never helps the situation. There is an ancient Hebrew proverb that says, "Fools give full vent to their rage, but the wise bring calm in the end."[1]

Four: In order to do number three, teach the family to call "time out" when they are angry. Imagine your son or daughter saying to you, "I'm angry, I've got to take a time-out." This means, "I need to cool off so I can talk calmly about this." Every family member respects the right of others to call a time-out.

Five: When you are taking a time-out, you are asking yourself, "Is this anger definitive or distorted? Did someone really treat me unfairly or did I simply not get what I wanted?" If I think my anger is definitive, then I need to be ready to say when I return from my time-out, "I'm angry because I think you treated me unfairly. May I explain?" If I think my anger is distorted, then I need to be ready to say, "I realize that I got angry because I did not get my way. May I explain?"

Six: Always be ready to listen to a family member who is angry. They have exhibited patience by taking a time-out. So we need to show patience by listening carefully as they share why they are angry. Don't interrupt them. Let them share fully what they are thinking and feeling and why.

Seven: Express understanding. You might say, "I think I understand what you are saying, and I can see why you would feel angry. If I were you, I would probably feel angry too." (And you would!)

Eight: Ask permission to share your perspective. "Now that I understand why you are angry, may I share my perspective?" You proceed to share what you meant by what you said, and why you said it, or why you took the action that stimulated their anger. Then ask, "Do you see where I was coming from? I did not intend to hurt you. I love you very much." If you know that what you did or said was unkind or unfair, then apologize and ask them to forgive you. You might also ask, "What can I do to make this right?"

Our objective is always to find a resolution so that our relationship can move forward. The steps above have helped many families learn how to process anger in a positive way. As parents, we must take the responsibility not only to learn to handle our own anger in a positive way, but to teach our children to do the same. Few social skills are more important than learning to exhibit patience when we experience anger. Mismanaged anger destroys marriages, hurts children, and fractures friendships.

"That's what we had to do—start somewhere. Nora grew up with parents who handled anger privately. I grew up in a family that seemed to stay angry," Antoine shared. "We had to find middle ground and see that anger, handled correctly, could actually be productive. Now we have teenagers, so they and we continue to get plenty of workouts in terms of managing anger. I guess you can say we're still under construction!"

I want to encourage you to establish an open-door policy with both the literal and emotional doors between you and your loved ones. Look for and follow through with opportunities to be patient with each other. Work with each other to resolve anger. Accept that anger is a normal, healthy, and potentially productive emotion. And allow yourself and your loved ones to have the emotional space, or freedom, you and they need to express appropriate anger. You likely have other ideas you may want to incorporate into your home improvement plan, but between yours and my ideas, you've got plenty to at least get the ball rolling!

DO-IT-YOURSELF

An open-door policy is only as inviting as the person on the other side of the open door. So how inviting are you? Do you patiently invite your loved ones into your emotional space to push through anger together? Or do you tend to shut them out and deal with anger on your own?

Think also about whether you make yourself available to your loved ones for support when they're angry, ignore their need for support altogether, or barge into their emotional space with your own anger. I know—that's a lot to think about, but these questions prompt you to increase your self-awareness. Healthy self-awareness, coupled with commitment to change and consistent effort, helps us successfully respond to anger with patience.

Of course, there are two sides to every door! Some of you are all for your own DIY makeover when it comes to anger and patience. But some of you are desperately waiting for your loved ones to deal with *their* anger in more effective ways. You'd love for them to hang a "welcome" sign on their door and become someone with whom you could work through anger. You're just not so sure that'll ever happen.

Although it can be discouraging to wait on someone else to make an effort to change, you don't have to wait on them in order to change yourself. You can choose to see and express anger differently. And you can replace your "warning" sign with an inviting "welcome" sign in an attempt to encourage your loved ones to work together through anger.

Whether or not your loved ones step up their own DIY efforts, don't stop with yours. You can't control them; you can only control yourself.

 ## ALL-IN BUDGET

Some people believe that anger will go away if they just don't talk about it. They close the door and hold their anger inside. This is never healthy. We are to seek to process anger as quickly as possible. If we hold anger inside and refuse to share with those at whom we are angry, the anger will turn to bitterness and later to hatred. Hatred wishes ill on the person with whom we are angry.

Anger that is held inside will eventually destroy families. Of course, one of the reasons many people take a "closed door" approach to anger is that they have been hurt in the past when they sought to share their feelings of anger with family members. Sometimes this can be traced to childhood where they were never allowed to express anger. If this was true of your childhood, I hope that this chapter will help you understand that there is a better way. We are influenced by our childhood, but we are not controlled by those unhealthy patterns of handling anger.

Obviously, the ideal place to start to create an open-door policy with regard to processing anger is in the marriage. I hope that you and your spouse are reading this book together. If so, then this chapter may be the beginning of a whole new way of handling anger. Then together you can teach your children a healthy way of understanding and processing anger. However, if you are a single parent and have experienced unresolved anger in the past, I hope that this chapter will give you a new perspective on anger management. Applying these principles with your children will be one of the most important things you do for their future success in life.

Another creative way of getting *all* your family members *all in* with increasing patience is to establish an open-door policy with both literal and emotional doors. You and they may need private time behind closed doors, but you don't have to slam doors or lock doors to keep each other out. Same with emotional doors. You don't have to emotionally shut each other out, and you don't have to impatiently attempt to shut down another family member's anger.

Lastly, your family can have fun talking about "welcome" and "warning" signs. Thank each other for handling anger in welcoming ways and for supporting each other in angry moments. Give each other permission to say, "I'm feeling angry; can we talk?" This kind of *all-in* effort and support not only helps couples and families increase patience but also helps us grow closer together.

SWEAT EQUITY

We don't have to work to be angry; anger happens naturally. Patience, on the other hand, doesn't come so easily; it requires a lot of work, or sweat equity. The payoff for that sweat equity is less shutting each other out and more inviting each other in for emotional support in angry times. We have to keep our eyes on that prize when pushing through anger together to become a more patient, supportive family.

In chapter 9, we've explored the home improvement tool of patience. The following recaps important tips for decreasing anger by increasing patience:

- **Don't shut each other out.** We don't always know how to break free from anger; it has a way of making us feel stuck. If we emotionally shut out our loved ones, they can't as easily help us get unstuck. But if we invite them into our anger, or appropriately share with them why we are angry, then they can listen, validate our feelings, encourage us, and help us gain perspective. They also can help us find solutions to whatever it is that's contributing to our anger.

- **Anger happens!** Anger is a natural, normal, healthy emotion. We don't need to deny anger. Instead, we need to find healthy ways to express anger. This requires that we give each other the emotional space needed to process angry thoughts and feelings.

- **Be productive, not destructive.** Needing and allowing emotional space, however, is not an excuse to be hurtful toward each other or to avoid working through anger. Dealing with anger can be challenging, but dealing with it openly and together increases our chances for productive outcomes.

- **Definitive or distorted anger?** Remember, definitive anger means someone mistreated you or spoke harshly to you. Distorted anger means that you simply did not get your way. They did nothing immoral; but what they said or did was not what you wanted to hear or see. While in your time-out, ask yourself, "Is my anger definitive or distorted?" If it is definitive, then you need to approach the person with, "I'm feeling angry, can we talk?" If it is distorted, then you need to say, "I'm feeling angry, and I realize that you did nothing wrong, but I would like to talk with you about why I'm angry." Either way, we are not holding anger inside. We are sharing it with the family member at whom we are angry.

- **Welcome or warning?** Patience is like a door with a "welcome" sign hanging on it; anger is like a door with a "warning" sign hanging on it. When we are angry, we can find patient, positive ways of interacting with and supporting each other. Patience draws us to one another; it encourages us to work together rather than emotionally shut each other out. Together, we can more effectively work through our anger rather than allowing our anger to push us apart.

 BIG REVEAL

Home improvement renovators often show us before and after pictures. This helps us remember what our homes looked like before and appreciate even more the amazing transformation that took place during the renovation.

Think about what's working and not working with your current handling of anger. Now, imagine a few weeks and months from now how your family might be more patient with each other in angry moments. Those "after pictures" are the big reveal moments you're working toward. Perhaps for you and your family, that will mean saying things like:

"I get it, you're mad. Talk to me. Help me understand."

"I need you to listen and understand where I'm coming from."

"I'm sorry I shut you out. If you're still willing to listen, I'd like to tell you how I'm feeling."

"Thank you for playing with me. That's all I wanted."

"Thank you for giving me some space. That's all I wanted."

"I'm here, whenever, if ever you want to talk."

"I love you no matter how angry you are, and I'm always willing to listen to you."

Patience may also be expressed through hugs, gentle touches, a listening ear, and a helping hand in moments of frustration. Keep an eye out for those types of big reveal moments, too. And be sure to thank each other every chance you get for less anger and more patience!

TALK IT OVER

1. In what ways do you make your loved ones feel welcome to talk about their anger? How do you discourage them from discussing it?

2. When have you and your loved ones been angry with each other over things that weren't really a big deal?

3. How lately have you or a loved one exercised patience with each other?

4. To better understand anger and how to respond to this potentially destructive emotion, read my book *Anger: Taming a Powerful Emotion*.

HOME IMPROVEMENT GOAL:
Replace disorganization.

HOME IMPROVEMENT TOOL:
Get organized.

Chapter 10

GETTING ORGANIZED

"Keep this, don't keep that." Decluttering our homes (and minds) frees up space we forgot we had.

> #yougottalaugh

GARY: "Where did you put my . . . ?" If only I had a dime for every time one of us said that! #Order in the court . . . and in our closets and drawers!

SHANNON: I'm not bossy, I'm a "master organizer"! #Order up, with a side of kindness!

GIVEN OUR LOVE of "stuff" in America, there's no surprise in the rise of commercial storage businesses and Goodwill stores. Our homes can't comfortably contain all our stuff, so we rent storage units or give it away.

When consulting with homeowners about creating more

space at home, one simple solution that home renovators and interior designers recommend is to declutter. This might mean getting rid of unneeded stuff or organizing it in a more effective way.

Clutter not only has a way of literally blocking our living space, but it also emotionally blocks, or discourages, some people from moving forward in life. For that reason, counselors, like home improvement specialists, sometimes encourage literal decluttering.

Literal decluttering is important, but more than that, I encourage couples and families to deal with the figurative "clutter" or disorganization with which so many of them struggle. "We never get anywhere on time." "We fight about who is supposed to be doing what." "It's too much. We can't keep up." Comments such as these reflect the frustration that disorganization can cause.

Disorganization happens often because life is busy. We can be fairly well organized with our time and energy, but it's still hard to "keep it all together" all the time. We overcommit, run behind, let some tasks slide to accomplish other unexpected duties, and sometimes take shortcuts to catch up. And yes, sometimes, we never catch up!

Disorganization also happens when we, as couples and parents, don't exert enough leadership. Instead, we think "it can wait" or "someone else will do it." The bad news, of course, is that with this kind of thinking, either everything doesn't get done, or everyone doesn't do their fair share of the work.

To assist couples and families who are stressed or

overwhelmed by disorganization, I encourage them to step up their leadership efforts. Before couples can lead their children, they must first clarify the source of disorganization. For example, some couples are overwhelmed because they do not have clearly defined roles—who will do what (childcare, paying bills, home maintenance, grocery shopping, food preparation, lawn care, car care, pet care, etc.). Each spouse brings unique strengths to the relationship and can use those strengths to help create and maintain order in the home.

In their role as parents, a couple can lead by being clear in their communication (chapter 6) but also more organized and consistent with how they lead their children. For example, routine is a great way of creating consistent schedules for children. Children then know what to expect and cooperate easier with things like bedtime, mealtime, baths, and homework.

Consistency with assigning and following through with household chores is another example of how parents can not only organize their home life but encourage their children's leadership development as well. Through assisting with chores and other cleanup or repair efforts, children learn the value of taking care of a home. They also get to see the value of teamwork.

In addition to stepping up leadership and teamwork, parents may need to cut back some of their family's unnecessary comings and goings. If work schedules can be changed to free up more time for the family—change schedules. If children need one less extracurricular activity— drop one activity. If trips to stores and doctors' offices can be consolidated—consolidate them. These are but a few examples of possible adjustments couples can make to decrease disorganization.

Of course, couples and families go through seasons of life in which disorganization is nearly unavoidable. If major changes can't be made in that particular season of life, then I encourage people to stress less, accept their circumstances as best they can, and be as flexible as they can with their various responsibilities and commitments.

Certainly, families' definition of disorganization and organization will vary widely, but generally speaking, most families function best when they have some level of organization, or order. Order is an important tool that couples and families need in their home improvement toolbox.

WHY ORGANIZATION?

Families are like businesses—to accomplish their shared goals, there must be leadership and order. Having been a part of a family and having worked for a business of one kind or another, you understand the importance of good leadership and order. Without it, couples and families, like businesses, falter; with it, they thrive.

Family therapists believe in the strength of a functional family structure. No matter the actual makeup of the family, children naturally look to their parents or other trusted caregivers to lead the way. Parents and caregivers, in turn, bear the natural responsibility of establishing order and providing a dependable, loving model in which their children can trust and thrive.

That's a lot of responsibility, isn't it?! To be good leaders. To create order. To be a functional family.

Whether self-imposed or other-imposed, creating and sustaining order can be stressful for parents. They feel the stress internally but also add to each other's stress by fussing at each other and by comparing themselves and their family to other families. "Why can't you guys get ready when I say it's time to get ready?" "Robert is always on time." "I bet *his* mom didn't forget to bring everyone a Valentine's card." "Their house always looks amazing."

Behind the fussing and comparing lies legitimate desire. After all, when you're actively raising your children, you hope you're doing it right. You pray, read books like this one, learn on the job, and hope for the best. Then, in what seems a blink of an eye, your children are grown, and you discover how well you did. Talk about big reveals!

Home improvement isn't a once-and-done project. In the case of disorganization and order, couples and families must continually adapt to their family's changing needs and schedules. That's another hallmark of a functional family—that it appropriately adjusts its roles and rules over time to effectively accommodate developmental changes. So keep your home improvement toolbox handy! As needs and schedules change, you and your spouse and children will have to increase order again and again to decrease disorganization.

DRAWING UP THE PLANS

In what areas of home life are you and your loved ones lacking order? Where do you need to step up your leadership to create and sustain order?

As you're working on your home improvement wish list, I recommend that you establish SMART goals.[1] You may have heard of SMART goals before. The acronym stands for: Specific, Measurable, Achievable, Reasonable, and Time-based.

To say, "I want us to be more organized" isn't specific enough. But saying, "I want us to arrive places on time" is specific. Now you have a target for which you and your family can aim.

Let's stick with that same goal of arriving on time. That's clearly measurable because you can, in fact, know whether your family is or is not on time. You may want to have a little fun together by keeping an "on time" chart with which you list your destinations and arrival times for each one.

Arriving on time is likely achievable, at least more times than not. If you find that the time you've allotted to get ready and leave is not enough time, then you might have to tweak your routine to have more time to get ready and leave in a timely manner.

If you notice that most other people are arriving on time for the same events, then you can probably comfortably assume the goal of arriving on time is reasonable.

Finally, time-based means that you and your family give yourselves a time frame to accomplish your desired goal. With our example goal, you might challenge yourselves, for starters, to arrive on time for one day, then one week, and then one month until you decide how well you've been able to consistently accomplish your goal.

Shannon suggested the "arriving on time" example because she's still working on that goal herself. She also likes to share with people another useful counseling tool—the Stages of Change Model.[2] This model consists of five stages: 1) In the pre-contemplation stage, people are not ready to make change. 2) In the contemplation stage, they're at least thinking about change. 3) In the preparation stage, they're now moving forward with plans for change. 4) In the action stage, they're actively implementing change. And 5) In the maintenance stage, change has set in and now must be maintained.

Shannon said, "I refer to the Stages of Change Model in counseling often because it helps me and others think more concretely about making realistic changes. If we're not ready for change, we're only frustrating ourselves by attempting to make unrealistic, unachievable goals."

How might SMART goals and the Stages of Change Model help you with your home improvement plans?

 # DO-IT-YOURSELF

Shannon is a do-it-yourselfer when it comes to order. "I really am a master organizer. I love to organize stuff, and I'm good at it. But wow, life is a formidable opponent when it comes to staying organized," she says.

Shannon's right! It's hard to stay organized all the time no matter how good you are at organization. So she does something very healthy—she is compassionate toward herself (chapter 8). This self-compassion helps her to be more flexible when her plans don't work out. That's the DIY project I want to encourage you to take on for yourself—flexibility!

With flexibility, you can still pursue order; you're just not as self-critical, and you don't stress out as much. You roll with life, and rather than try to accomplish perfect order, you celebrate the perfectly imperfect order you and your loved ones are able to accomplish in that season of life.

"We have a lot going on, and that's a good thing," Shannon says. "I regularly tell people that I'm good and tired because no matter how tired I am of keeping up with our busy schedules, I'm still good—I really am."

Shannon's positive attitude carries over into her family life. In fact, I laughed when she shared with me the little song she made up. They often sing it when they're running late for school:

"We've got a shot. Doesn't happen a lot. But we've got a shot. Today is our day!"

As you, too, work on finding the order that works best for your family, I encourage you be flexible with your plans. And remember, you do indeed always have a shot of accomplishing your home life goals. Making SMART goals and being realistic about change will help you!

ALL-IN BUDGET

As we were writing this book, Shannon and her family were selling their house and building a new one. This was yet another great test of not only her organizational abilities but also of Stephen's and their children's. Pulling off this major transition definitely required an *all-in* effort.

"In preparation for showing the house, we boxed up a lot of stuff we didn't use on a regular basis, and that all filled up half our garage. Or at least we thought we didn't use that stuff regularly. Over the next several months of waiting for our house to sell, we brought stuff back and forth from the garage between showings.

"The showings, themselves, added extra stress. On top of our normally busy schedules, we were now trying either to keep the house clean and organized or running home quickly to prep it before a last-minute showing."

Perhaps you can relate to Shannon and her family's stress. They were dealing with both literal clutter (all the stuff they moved to the garage) and figurative clutter (the additional disorganization that transitional living can cause).

"As organized as I attempted to be, we routinely were searching for a lost this or that. We even accidentally threw away a check and lost Avery's cellphone during that time. We were embarrassed but asked the person to write and resend the check, and eventually, we found Avery's phone buried in the couch."

Despite the stress of searching for and losing things,

Shannon's family maintained a positive, helpful attitude. They patiently worked together to clean the house and store their belongings for showings. They prayed together for God's will for their family. And they rolled with life as they waited for God to work out the details.

"Selling our house took way longer than we anticipated, and to be honest, it was really stressful at times. I was so proud of my crew. They truly were ***all in*** when it came to rolling with the chaos that comes along with moving."

Whatever your family's challenges, you and they, like the Wardens, will need an ***all-in*** effort. To encourage everyone's involvement, I recommend that you: 1) step up your leadership, 2) give your children opportunities for age-appropriate leadership, 3) be clear about the order you want to implement, and 4) find the right balance of pursuing your organization goals and being flexible with yourself and your loved ones when you or they fall short of those goals.

SWEAT EQUITY

When we declutter our house, we free up space we may have forgotten we had. Similarly, we're less stressed and free up mental space when we "declutter" our schedules and goals. In both cases, we get to say "keep this, don't keep that." Making intentional, life-changing choices like that can feel really good! But as with all home improvement, to create and sustain more order in our lives, we're going to have to put in the sweat equity.

In chapter 10, we've explored the home improvement tool of order. The following is a recap of important tips for decreasing disorganization and increasing order:

- **Let go of some stuff!** We really do have a lot of stuff, don't we?! Our minds and schedules are equally "stuffed"—stuffed with all the goals we are trying to accomplish and with the stress that our goal-chasing can often cause. Your home renovator or interior designer may advise you to cut back on or better organize your literal stuff. Me? I'm encouraging you to, if possible, let go of some of your over-packed schedule and impossible goal-chasing. Letting go of this kind of "stuff" can be very stress-relieving.

- **Roll with it!** It may be that you are simply in a busy season of life and can't cut back on schedules and goals right now. Be compassionate toward yourself and your family by accepting the season you're in and being as flexible as you can be with things like promptness to meetings, missed deadlines, forgotten laundry, and fluctuating bedtimes. Exercising compassion and flexibility will help reduce your stress.

- **Step up!** As an "executive" of your family, you're in charge of leading your family by creating and managing order in the home. Before you can lead your children, you and your spouse both have to step up your leadership contribution and support of each other. The "business" goes the way of the leaders, so it won't cut it to say "someone else will do it." You are the someone else.

- **Give your children leadership opportunities.** By setting consistent routines, delegating age-appropriate chores, and including your children in home upkeep, you're giving them leadership training opportunities. Through these training experiences, your children can learn the value of caring for their home and the value of teamwork.

- **Try SMART goals for a change.** Saying "I wish we could be more organized" is not specific, measurable, achievable, reasonable, or time-based enough. The SMARTer your goals, the better! You also need to take into account how ready for change you and your family are. With SMART goals and the right stage of readiness, you and they have a real shot at creating and sustaining more order in your day-to-day lives.

 ## BIG REVEAL

What will decreased disorganization and increased order look and sound like in your family? Perhaps something like this . . .

"We've been on time every day this week!"

"I forgot show-and-tell was today, but fortunately, my kindergartener reminded me in time. We found something in the car that he could share!"

"We got homework done and baths finished early enough that we were able to read before bedtime. I can't believe it!"

"My husband voluntarily does most of the grocery shopping. For that and so many other reasons, he really is the best 'business partner' I could have married."

"It was my job to take the kids to sports practices this afternoon, make dinner, and get homework started. I don't know how my wife does it all, but I'm more and more grateful."

"Taking a season off from sports gave our family some much-needed downtime."

These, of course, are just examples of near-future big reveals that I hope you and your family get to enjoy together. You and they will need to work together to decide what more order will actually look like for your family. I can't define and design what your organization should look like, and you can't fairly judge your family by another family's level of organization. However, by setting and steadily working together toward realistic goals, you will begin to see and feel the change for which you're hoping. And that's what matters most—that you and your family create and live by the order that makes the most sense for you.

TALK IT OVER

1. In what ways are you disorganized? What about your family?

2. What changes have you and your family already made to create more order at home? What changes still need to be made?

3. What's one order-related goal that you want your family to aim for? Apply the SMART goals acronym to that goal to increase your odds of successfully accomplishing the goal.

· · · · · · · · · · ·

HOME IMPROVEMENT GOAL:
Eliminate boredom.

HOME IMPROVEMENT TOOL:
Create fun.

· · · · · · · · · · ·

Chapter 11

CREATING FUN

What good are city parks, walking trails, toys, and games if we don't actually use them?

#yougottalaugh

GARY: I'm fun, just not nearly as fun as Karolyn. With her, every day is an adventure! #Fun keeps you young at heart!

SHANNON: Our kids aren't fanatics—they're fun-atics! If they're awake, they're having fun. #Fun makes life interesting!

REMEMBER ALL THE FUN you had as a child? Those were the good old days, weren't they?! You weren't stressed out or tired. You had all the time in the world to do what you did best—be a kid!

To children, potential for fun is everywhere and in everything. Bike rides, snow days, and leaf piles represent great opportunities for fun. Blank pages, crayons, scissors, and glue invite limitless, imaginative creations. Dolls, stuffed animals, action figures, and die-cast cars become real, living characters to be cared for, dressed up, fought, and crashed. And the jokes, riddles, noises, and silly faces—children's energy and love of fun is pretty amazing!

As we become adults, we still love fun. Our energy and opportunities for fun and our definition of fun just changes a little. Fun for us might be relaxing in our favorite chair while reading a book or watching a movie, or doing water aerobics or taking a brisk walk. You might also spend time laughing with your spouse or kids. Finding time for fun may be difficult when we are dealing with real people who have real needs that keep us busy seemingly around the clock, but we definitely won't have fun if we don't try.

Interestingly, even though adults and children have different perspectives on fun, we both often get bored if we get stuck in a rut. This is a problem for couples and families as well. When we do the same things over and over every day, we can become bored with life and desire new and exciting experiences.

To change things at home, couples and parents often think about how they can better use fun places in and around their homes. They want to create new, fun, and relaxing spaces or expand and update existing spaces for relaxation and recreation. Whether done by home renovators and interior designers or by do-it-yourselfers, a long list of possibilities emerges. Inside, they may consider reading nooks, game rooms, and man caves. Outside, they may consider swings, tree houses, sandboxes, outdoor eating spaces, fire pits, basketball courts, gardens . . . you get the idea.

Fun is the easiest-to-use home improvement tool of all. In fact, you'll probably want to make extra room in your toolbox for this boredom-busting home improvement tool!

HAVE FUN!

I want you to consider increasing fun in your home life for three reasons. First is the reality that life is much more than work. Yes, work can be fun, and I wish that for you— that you enjoy your work! But it is too easy for many of us to get caught up in our work and focus only on making ends meet. C. S. Lewis wrote, "My father, whom I implicitly believed, represented adult life as one of incessant drudgery under the continual threat of financial ruin."[1]

You too may have grown up in a home that for one reason or another didn't value or prioritize fun. Or you may now be the grownup who favors financial peace, or an orderly house, over fun. But the good news

> Your spouse and children may wish you would play and relax more.

is that fun doesn't have to be expensive. Many families find or create free, fun experiences or save up to be able to afford more expensive adventures. If you open your mind to the value of increased fun, you'll find a way to make fun happen and thus enjoy life even more.

A second reason for considering how to increase your family's fun time is that your loved ones are waiting for you! Much like C. S. Lewis, your spouse and children may wish you would play and relax more. They often invite you to engage with them in play of one kind or another, and you continue to say things like, "In a minute," "I can't right now," or "Next time, I promise." If you find yourself too often turning down invitations for fun with your loved ones, you need to consider making changes in your schedule and in your attitude about quality time. Otherwise, you could be guilty of putting your loved ones at the end of the line.

On the other hand, it could be that *you're* the one who's at the end of the line. Perhaps you're waiting for your spouse or older children to engage with you in fun activities. I know from working with many people that it can be sad and discouraging to keep hoping that your loved ones will come around. One father said, "I wish my son would just try playing golf with me. I think he would like it." My encouragement to you is, don't give up! Continue inviting them, but don't pressure them. You may even need to take more of an interest in their fun activities. If they won't join you, then you can join them.

Of course, joining in with your loved ones in their fun doesn't mean you shouldn't pursue your own fun interests. In fact, that's the third reason to increase play and fun—you deserve it! Think about how you feel when you make time for fun. Whether that means taking a pottery class, running during your lunch break, writing poetry, or taking relaxing bubble baths, fun refuels you! It not only is good for you emotionally and physically, fun also spills over into your relationships as well. You have more energy to invest in your family.

DRAWING UP THE PLANS

How do you want to increase fun at home? Remember, I'm not a home renovator, so I'm not able to advise you on how to improve your literal space; I'm a marriage and family counselor and am encouraging you to look for ways you can increase fun in your family's life.

Shannon and I are fans of the practical. So for starters, as you plan for more fun, let's look at your family's typical routine. Can you fit more fun into your breakfast routine perhaps by having a joke book in your kitchen? Can you make the trip to school and work more fun by singing or listening to stories on CD or podcast? Can you take a walk during lunch? Can you and your family cook supper together and perhaps change up your menus to include international recipes—dinner from around the world?

What about family playtimes? Children naturally play and want you to join in. What if you committed at least thirty minutes every day to play with your kids with no interruptions?

When our children were young, they loved to play board games: Monopoly or Scrabble. Today's children may prefer video games. I personally think that board games stimulate much more mental and social growth. However, the important thing is that you are playing with them. "Stephen and I are tired from work and don't always feel like playing," Shannon says, "but we jump in and play as often as we can. And, whether that's playing Monopoly, having pirate fights, or playing restaurant, we and the kids have fun together."

What about exercise time? Many adults don't feel like they have time to exercise. But what if you incorporate your children into your exercise time by taking them on walks and bike rides with you? You, of course, would have a harder time involving your children, especially younger children, with more intense workouts, but that may be a time for your child-free fun. You may need help from your spouse to care for your kids while you make much-needed exercise time ("fun" time) for yourself. Even shooting hoops, playing Wiffle ball, or passing the football with your family can be personally rewarding.

Bedtimes are another potential fun time. Reading to your children, allowing them to read to you, reading for yourself after the children are in bed, and reading to your spouse are all fun possibilities. Other possibilities include singing, making up silly songs, drawing, or making a fun snack together.

Remember to add "fun couple time" to your home improvement plans.

As you can see from this short, sample list of ideas for increasing fun and play, you don't need special places in your home to have fun. Those spaces can certainly inspire fun, but the main requirement for increasing fun is intentionality. In fact, as humans, we are hardwired for fun. Like our children and grandchildren automatically do, we as adults just have to give in to play!

Before leaving the "drawing board," I've reminded you

to make fun time for yourself and fun time with your children. I also want to put in an extra plug for fun time with your spouse. I've talked with thousands of couples over time who had little time and energy left for each other after handling all their other responsibilities. Instead of giving each other their best selves, they got each other's leftovers. They needed more time and fun together. You and your spouse need the same thing, so remember to add fun "couple time" to your home improvement plans.

DO-IT-YOURSELF

Because I tend to be a workaholic, I have to schedule fun time. Karolyn helps me with this. She stays busy herself but incorporates fun in her daily life better than I do. So when she says, "Let's take a trip" or "Let's go out to eat," I say, "Where and when?" Not only do I enjoy our time together, but I also enjoy the downtime for myself.

Shannon admits that she, too, gets caught up at times in work. "I will be busy working and hear Stephen playing video games or having pirate fights with the kids. He is way more fun than me and inspires me to stop what I'm doing and enjoy the moment."

These are DIY examples of how Shannon and I are trying to give ourselves to fun and to play more often. What about you? How do you need to do it yourself and have more fun?

What if you let yourself go, if you were to surprise your spouse or children by engaging them in a fun activity? Try it and see what happens! Ask your spouse if he or she wants to watch a television show together. Ask your children if they want to color or play basketball together. Choose for yourself to have a cup of tea while you read a favorite magazine.

These are just a few examples to get you thinking. You know your family's needs and interests. Why not embrace new opportunities for fun? If your loved ones ask why, or if you're asking why—the answer is "just because." Just because there's way more to life than work, because your loved ones are waiting on you to engage them and enjoy life together, and because you need and deserve to have fun.

As Carlos said of his and Natalia's DIY efforts, "it's the best thing we ever did for ourselves and for our family— have more fun! Granted, fun didn't come nearly as natural as work did, but we started scheduling fun, and things started changing for the better."

ALL-IN BUDGET

Children don't really need help increasing their fun. Watch and listen to them for just a few minutes, and you'll see what I mean. Adults, on the other hand, sometimes need help in the fun and play category of home improvement. Normally, I would say, "Ask your children for help." However, when it comes to fun, asking your kids for help may set you up for burnout. Yet you'll need accountability to encourage follow-through on your plans for increasing fun.

In light of your need for accountability, I recommend that you go ***all-in*** on fun by making yourself a Fun Chart. This chart should include three categories: 1) family fun, 2) couple fun, and 3) me fun. You can rename or reorder these categories at your discretion. You also can post this list publicly and let your spouse and children help cheer you on in your efforts. That's my recommendation—that you post your list on the refrigerator or somewhere visible to the whole family. Make it colorful, preferably involving stickers or gold stars! This will invite them to support your ***all-in*** effort and encourage them, as well, that fun is welcomed and valued in your home. Of course, you may also choose to keep your Fun Chart private, but whether publicly or privately, still give yourself checks every time you accomplish your daily or weekly "fun goals." And allow for spontaneity. Some of us "planners" need encouragement to break away from the schedule and do something on the spur of the moment. That in itself can be fun!

What will your fun goals be? That's totally up to you! You might choose from any of the ideas I've already shared, but you'll likely come up with fun goals that are specific and relevant to your life. Here's where SMART goals (chapter 10) will again come in handy. By setting meaningful but doable fun goals, you're more likely to follow through and make forward progress. As you take small steps each day toward accomplishing your fun goals, give yourself checks or smiley faces for effort. Yes, this is very "kindergarten," but it worked then, and it'll work now! Give it a try! And one last encouragement: keep your Fun Chart fun!

SWEAT EQUITY

Having more fun will be the easiest "sweat equity" you and your loved ones will ever put into home improvement. Why? Because you all want and need more fun time individually, as a couple, and as a family. The biggest challenge won't be the fun itself but the intentionality you as an adult will need to exert to free your mind and your schedule for fun. If you can pull off that intentional effort, you and your loved ones will see a decrease in boredom and an increase in fun.

In chapter 11, we've explored the home improvement tool of fun. The following is a recap of important tips for decreasing boredom and increasing fun:

- **Be a fun-atic!** Children specialize in fun—they're not fan-atics; they're fun-atics! We as adults know . . . we used to be children! Understandably, as our responsibilities increased, many of us lost time, energy, and opportunity for fun. Our definition of fun also changed. But we still want and need fun. If we get stuck in the same old same old, we become bored. To decrease that boredom, we have to bring back the fun in our lives. This is where we can take a page from our children and grandchildren's book. We need to give ourselves freely to fun and to play.

- **Follow through on fun.** Knowing we want or need more fun isn't enough to create change; we have to follow through on those thoughts and feelings. This may mean participating more in playtime with our children, taking more walks with our spouse, and making time to do something fun for ourselves that's not work-related. Following through on fun energizes us and has the bonus benefit of giving us increased energy for our most important relationships.

- **Do it for yourself.** You deserve to have fun. Period. That's enough of a reason to give fun a chance. You work hard, take care of your family, and tend to put yourself last in most every way. What if, for once, you gave yourself permission to have fun—to rest, exercise, read, write, paint, sew, play golf, join a choir, plant a garden—whatever it is you do for fun! I believe you'll quickly see and feel the results. You may even recognize that good feeling from years gone by when you had less responsibility. That good feeling is still there and still worthwhile; you just need to allow yourself time and opportunity to experience it.

- **Fun is feasible.** Stop making excuses! Fun doesn't have to be expensive; it doesn't have to take a lot of time. Sometimes we put off fun for no good reason. Granted, being tired is a reasonable excuse. But that's my point! If you're too tired to have fun, you need to fix that. Get some rest, and get busy making time to have fun by yourself, with your children, and with your spouse.

- **Just because.** You technically don't need a reason to have fun. I've given you reasons: 1) there's more to life than work, 2) your loved ones are waiting for you to engage in fun with them, and 3) you deserve to have fun. But really, you and your loved ones should have as much fun as possible—just because. Fun is an important part of life that refuels us and challenges us to keep testing our abilities and imaginations. Having fun with our family makes fun all the sweeter!

- **Fun Chart.** It may seem a little "old school," but when it comes to having fun, a Fun Chart is just what the doctor ordered. Whether you post your chart for the family to see or keep it private, challenge yourself on a daily and/ or weekly basis to create time and follow through on: 1) family fun, 2) couple fun, and 3) me fun. You can rename or reorder these categories at your choosing, but give a Fun Chart a chance. Let it help you organize your goals and serve as both a source of accountability and a reward system. As you accomplish your fun goals, I suggest you reward yourself with more fun!

 ## BIG REVEAL

There's no reason you can't have fun today. Sing, dance, laugh, color, build something, watch a favorite show, read, let your child read to you— have fun today. Today is a key word. You can't go back in time and have fun. You also can't put off fun until you accomplish all your other goals. Today's your chance.

As you give fun a chance, I believe you'll see and feel many big reveal moments in which you and your loved ones aren't doing the same old thing. Instead, you and they will, together, feel the energy and satisfaction that comes from fun. Your adult definition of fun will, of course, be different than your children's definition. Your definition may even differ from your spouse's definition. Let your differences encourage you to try new things. Fun is still fun, and it energizes us and draws us together. Not only are the opportunities for fun endless, so, too, are the big reveal moments fun creates. Enjoy!

TALK IT OVER

1. How are you already working to create more fun in your life?

2. When was the last time you and your spouse had fun together?

3. When was the last time you and your kids had fun together?

4. What's your children's idea of fun?

5. What's your spouse's idea of fun?

6. What current fun goals should you add to your Fun Chart?

HOME IMPROVEMENT GOAL:
Decrease distraction.

HOME IMPROVEMENT TOOL:
Build connection.

Chapter 12

BUILDING CONNECTION

The kitchen is the heart of the home; connection is the heartbeat.

> #yougottalaugh

GARY: With some calls, a loss of cellphone connection is a well-timed blessing! Never with Karolyn though!
#Connection keeps us together.

SHANNON: Remember connecting the dots as a kid? I think I'm still "connecting the dots"—the "big picture" kinds of dots.
#Connection for life!

EVER HEARD SOMEONE say, "I want a beautiful new kitchen with plenty of room for one person"? Me neither! More typically, when dreaming of their ideal kitchen, people say something like, "I want us all to be able to sit together, see each other, and talk to each other when we eat."

Why? Because as couples and families, we crave connection. We want and need to be together physically and "together" emotionally.

Kitchens bring us together. That's where the food is, and that's where each of us finds not only physical nourishment but also emotional nourishment! For these reasons, the kitchen is known as the heart of our home. The connection that takes place there is our heartbeat—it keeps us going!

Of course, connection can happen anytime, anywhere. Yet, the kitchen is an important central gathering place that invites us to share life and build connection. Beyond bringing us together to eat, the kitchen is where we unload and store groceries, decide on menus, prepare meals, and clean up after meals. Families might also hold family meetings and do homework around the kitchen table. No wonder we call it "the heart" of our homes!

However, just being in the kitchen doesn't magically create connection between us and our loved ones. For that matter, I've worked with many people who lived in the same home but were emotionally disconnected. At his father's funeral, a young man recently said to me, "I never knew my Dad, even though we lived in the same house."

DISTRACTED AND DISCONNECTED

Sure, we all desire emotional closeness. But we have to put forth the intentional effort needed to accomplish and sustain that connection. Without the ingredients of desire and effort, distractions easily pop up and pull our attention away from our most important relationships.

Chen and Kiera committed as newlyweds to prioritize family life, but that priority eventually gave way to numerous other priorities. As their family grew, they continued to have desire for family time but had less and less energy and opportunity for quality time together. They knew something had to change if they were ever going to regain a healthy family focus.

Distraction is a problem for many families and, like connection, can happen anytime, anywhere. Sometimes distraction is an unavoidable part of life. Often, however, couples fail to guard themselves from avoidable distractions. We're on our phones, managing our calendars, planning our to-do lists, worrying about things that are out of our control, or busy doing everything but prioritizing our family.

When distraction becomes the norm, we take each other for granted (chapter 3) and treat each other as housemates who will always be there no matter how we treat each other. That's a problem that, left uncorrected, will create emotional distance. We get too good at checking out emotionally when we should be lovingly and consistently checking in with each other.

Instead of ignoring each other, what if we learned to prioritize our relationships? What if we learned to see each other as valuable teammates in life? "I need you in my life!" "I don't know what I'd do without you!" Heartfelt sentiments such as these reflect the emotional closeness that's possible when we as couples and families decrease distraction.

To accomplish that home improvement goal, we need the home improvement tool of connection.

CONNECTION: NOW IS THE TIME!

Life is short! Why is it then that so many of us go through life "checking the boxes" and "going through the motions"? We rush everywhere but home, give our best self to the world instead of our families, and "put off until tomorrow" what we could and should be doing today. All the while missing opportunities for connection with our loved ones.

The day-to-day check-ins around the kitchen table are important for building emotional closeness, but do we really see and feel the value that we bring to each other's lives? We can't afford to merely check the boxes in life; our loved ones are here now, and now is the time we get to enjoy life together.

Shannon shares, "My dad died June 24, 2017. He had just turned seventy-three. I think about him every day, and often find myself tearing up because I miss him and wish I had made better use of my time with him. I'm sad, too, because I wish my children could have had more time to know him and be known by him."

Shannon knows even better than before the value of deep connection with family. Death has that power about it—it reminds us of how short life is.

Karolyn and I have known for a while the shortness of life. We know we're in the final quarter of our lives, and, rather than grieving lost time, we've recommitted ourselves to connecting with our children and grandchildren in much greater ways than before. We regularly check in with them to keep up with their joys and struggles and to offer to help in any way that we can. But more than this, we've made it a point to go on trips and have fun with them as often as possible. Why? Because we know time is short! We don't want to miss our chance to connect in truly meaningful ways while we're all still here together.

Emotional connection opens the door to the possibility of helping each other reach our goals and purposes in life. We are all wired differently. We have different personalities, abilities, and interests. When we are distracted with our own toys, we live in isolation. When we are connected, we enter into each other's lives and can encourage each other. A young man once said to me, "I love playing football, but my father never comes to my games. He is always too busy at work." For this father, work keeps him disconnected from his son's interests.

We believe that life's greatest satisfaction is found in serving God by serving others. Jesus said about Himself, "I did not come to be served, but to serve." He is our model. Upon receiving the Nobel Prize, Dr. Albert Schweitzer, a physician who invested his life in Africa said, "I am convinced that the only ones who will find true happiness in life are those who seek and find how to serve others."

One of our goals in family life is to help each other develop our abilities and discover ways to serve others. This is not likely to happen if we are not emotionally connected.

> **We realize that we're doing life together for a reason.**

Pursuing our calling or our dreams brings meaning to our individual lives but also adds meaning to our home life. You and your spouse and children each have desires and abilities to contribute to each other and to the world. When we as couples and families make this connection, we learn to see each other and relationships with each other as purpose-filled. We realize that we're doing life together for a reason—to encourage each other as we fulfill our individual and collective purposes.

Deep connection and purpose-filled relationships are life-changing and relationship-changing ways of improving our home life. When connecting at this level, you and your loved ones not only share an address, but you and they share in each other's purpose in life.

DRAWING UP THE PLANS

You may be asking, "So you want us to connect and experience purpose-filled relationships?" Yes! That's exactly right. You and your loved ones naturally want and need connection. Connection with our family truly is the emotional nourishment that sustains us in life.

You also may be asking, "Doesn't being a family connect us? Do we really have to do anything more than that?" Another good question! We can't just hope that sharing the same name or same address creates connection. Many couples and families go through the motions of life without ever fully allowing themselves to enjoy each other. As your home life improvement consultant, I want more for you! I want your home improvement plan to involve greater connection, and thus, greater joy and purpose than you and your loved ones have previously experienced.

How do we create deeper connection? For starters, you'll need to assess your home life for distractions. What keeps you from connecting with each other? Perhaps you want to follow Common Sense Media's "device-free dinner"[1] advice and put away your digital devices during mealtimes. It may seem awkward at first. The kids may even resist this change. Explain your purpose in making this change. You might say, "We want to use our mealtimes to share our lives with each other. We want to know what each of us is doing and how we might help each other."

To give some structure to your mealtime conversation you may want to use Shannon's suggestion. She recommends that you try "three things, three minutes." Ask each other: 1) What happened today? 2) Why is it important to you? 3) How do you feel about it? You may talk about only one thing that happened that day or about several. You may talk for three minutes or thirty minutes. The main goal with "three things, three minutes" is that your family find doable, meaningful ways of connecting.

You may also want to agree that, at any time one of you needs to talk or be heard, one or more of you will stop whatever you're doing to support that loved ones need. Moves like these clearly show your commitment to connection.

The distractions that we feel as couples and families aren't always time-related. Some distractions are related to the many worries or concerns that we face in life. Among these worries are loss of friends, change of classes or schools, fear of failure, job-related stressors, financial strain, sickness, death of a loved one . . . the list goes on. Supporting each other as we work through our concerns is a powerful way couples and families demonstrate our commitment to connection.

One creative solution Shannon and I recommend to couples and families when dealing with worry is to create a family worry or concern box. (I prefer the word "concern" rather than "worry." Concern leads to action, while worry tends to leave us overwhelmed with no answers.) If I am concerned about my upcoming exam, then I am motivated to study. If I am worried, I simply feel overwhelmed and afraid I will fail the exam. The concern box can be any size. Family members write down their concerns and place the slips of paper in the box. Other family members may periodically read the concerns and pray for their loved one. Periodically, we may have family time when each person gets to share one of their concerns and family members express empathy, and perhaps offer suggestions. This is a supportive way of connecting with each other.

Whatever your family's distractions and whatever your home improvement plans, I encourage you to remember that, although connection requires action, connection is an attitude. You need to learn to recognize that life is short, that time with each other is valuable, and that you and they have the amazing privilege of supporting each other as you each live out your purpose in life.

DO-IT-YOURSELF

Encouraging and helping others should be a way of life. Our family should be at the top of the list of people we encourage and help. Give some thought to how you are gifted and how you might help others.

One way you can know your purpose is to ask yourself, "What brings me the most joy?" That likely is your unique calling or the dream that propels you forward. Focus on this calling or dream, train for it, develop it, refine it, take great joy in it, and eagerly await its effect on others.

People often ask me, "Gary, how have you managed to write fifty-plus books?" Honestly, I didn't set out to write books. I sought to help people as a counselor. The books are an overflow of my counseling. I just kept going, following God's calling in my life to write and help people. One book led to another, and before I knew it, I'm here, writing and encouraging you toward home improvement. And I still love it after all this time!

That's what I hope for you, that you do it yourself! Listen for your purpose, take the next step and then the next, until you have challenged yourself and helped as many people along the way as you can. I hope, like me, you can someday look back with great joy at how your life influenced others. I also hope you will be grateful for those who influenced and helped you. Those connections will have been your most important contributions over your lifetime.

ALL-IN BUDGET

Many people say, "I don't know how to talk to my family." "I can barely get my teenager to talk to me about his day, let alone his hopes and dreams."

Talking can be challenging, and the phrase "deep connection" may even be a little scary to some folks. You may want to say, instead, something like, "I care about you and about your future, and I want to support you every way I can." The good news is that you don't necessarily need to announce your plans to connect; you can just get busy decreasing distractions, listening more intently, telling each other more often how much you value them, and generally supporting each other through seasons of life and the challenges you face along the way. This effort in itself may motivate your family to follow suit. The good news is that your simplest efforts in this area can encourage family members of all ages.

The need for practical ways of connecting motivated Dr. Ramon Presson and me to coauthor the two books: *101 Conversation Starters for Couples*[2] and *101 Conversation Starters for Families*.[3] These books are simply a collection of questions that will stimulate communication. Books like these are great to have lying around in the gathering places of your home, but you can also use "three things, three minutes" as a way of getting conversation going and cultivating connection between you, your spouse, and your children.

You might also trade off conversation leadership duties at times so that you each take turns asking each other about your day or about other items of interest.

Wherever you and your family gather, and whether or not you go with the "three things, three minutes" approach, the more time you give to connection, the greater impact you will have on each other. As you talk together more frequently and more in-depth, you will also have opportunities to support each other in your unique purposes in life.

 ## SWEAT EQUITY

Kitchen renovations are among some of the most costly home improvements. Fortunately, connection isn't nearly as expensive! In fact, the hard work of connection isn't so hard after all. Why? Because the *action* of connection starts with an *attitude* of connection. Realizing each other's value starts in our hearts and then leads us to prioritize our relationships, spend time with each other, share with and listen to each other, and encourage one another. This type of investment will live on forever as one generation passes along to the next the importance of connection. Talk about return on investment! What could be greater?

In chapter 12, we've explored the home improvement

tool of connection. The following is a recap of important tips for decreasing distraction and increasing connection:

- **Connection brings us together.** As we've already said, a shared address or last name does not guarantee emotional closeness. To cultivate connection between us and our spouse and children, we have to prioritize our relationships over life's distractions. That may mean taking steps such as turning off our devices during family times and truly expressing interest in each other's daily lives. We may also need to better support each other during stressful or otherwise hard times and encourage one another more as we each seek to fulfill our unique purposes in life.

- **Distractions happen.** Life is full of distractions, many of which can be minimized in order to enhance family life. All families need to keep a check on how well they're decreasing unnecessary distractions. It's especially important that the adults take the lead in this area and, for that matter, in all home improvement efforts. As couples prioritize each other more, and as parents prioritize family time more, the children will follow suit. This is not a once-and-done effort. Expect regular recommitment in the area of connection because distractions happen and can quickly contribute to emotional distance in the home.

- **Enjoy!** If you're just checking boxes or going through the motions of life, what are you waiting for? Life is passing you by, which means time with your loved ones is, too. After Shannon's dad died, her mom commented, "I look around and see the things he used to worry about—bills, the house—and none of it matters to him anymore." We all have to keep up our day-to-day responsibilities, but in the big picture, we shouldn't put off today what we might not be able to do tomorrow. Love your family today! Live life to its fullest today, while you can!

- **Start now!** There truly is no time like the present when it comes to connection. Your family may be caught off guard a bit, but start now—listening, asking them about their day and about their interests and goals, and telling them you are rooting for them and praying for them. The more you and they make time for emotional closeness, the more natural it will become for your family. This type of relational investment can and likely will become one that far outlives your lifetime as your children and their children pass along the gift of connection across the generations.

- **Live purpose-filled.** Distractions not only keep us from seeing and supporting our loved ones' unique purposes in life; they also keep us from fulfilling ours. Busyness and juggling all our responsibilities can easily sidetrack us from following our unique calling or dreams. Allow yourself to once again, and more clearly than ever, hear the leading you feel in your life. What is it that you want to be doing to live a more meaningful life and fulfill your unique purpose? What are you waiting for? Now's your chance!

- **Three things, three minutes.** For fun, introduce this activity to your family. This is a creative way of relieving the pressure to talk by offering a simple but concrete way of responding. The "three things" are: 1) What happened today? 2) Why is it important to you? 3) How do you feel about it? It could be that your kids answer the "What happened today" question with great detail. If so, then listen for which event might lend itself to asking questions two and three. The main goal is to get each other sharing, and as you may have heard, "Sharing is caring!" I'd go one step further: "Sharing is caring and preparing!" When we share in each other's lives, we're better able to support each other, or help each other prepare for our various purposes in life.

- **Father–son connection.** My friend Dr. Clarence Shuler and I wrote a book for young men, ages 11–16, titled *Choose Greatness: 11 Wise Decisions That Brave Young Men Make.*[4] In the introduction, we encourage young men to read the book with their father or another adult male mentor. If you have a son, consider reading through this book and talking it through together.

 ## BIG REVEAL

"You believed in me before I believed in myself."

"I could always count on you to be there for me."

"Thanks, Mom and Dad, for all the time you spent with us."

"Thank you, Honey, for putting our relationship first."

Imagine you and your family saying words like these to each other twenty years from now. But why wait? What if you and your loved ones began to connect now in greater ways such that in a matter of months, you and they began to notice the difference?

To accomplish your desire for greater connection, you will need to decrease the various unnecessary distractions that create emotional distance between you. More than that, you can start changing your attitude from one of disregard to one of purpose-filled living. You and your family can begin to see one another's value and support one another's unique purposes in ways that draw you together like never before.

One last reminder. If you don't put in the necessary sweat equity, you can't accomplish your home improvement plan for increased connection. No work, no big reveal! Grab your home improvement toolbox and get to work!

 # TALK IT OVER

1. What unnecessary distractions tend to disrupt your family time? How have you and your family already begun working on decreasing those distractions?

2. What worries are you and/or your family facing right now that distract you from giving yourselves as fully to your relationships with each other?

3. How have you and your family supported each other during worrisome or otherwise hard times in life?

4. How do you and your family express appreciation for each other?

5. How are you working to fulfill your unique purpose(s)?

Epilogue:

HOME MAINTENANCE

Home maintenance and home life require lots of do-overs.

#yougottalaugh

GARY: From mowing the grass to cleaning toilets and vacuuming floors—who knew houses took so much work? #Home maintenance is never done.

SHANNON: Marks on the walls, crumbs, and sock lint no matter how often I sweep or vacuum, dirty dishes in the sink . . . our home is very . . . "lived in." #Home maintenance varies in quality from home to home.

"I CAN'T BELIEVE IT! That's not the same house!"

Often you'll hear that exclamation. This is a common homeowner expression after a major home improvement project. But in actuality, although people are amazed at the transformation their home has undergone, it is, in fact, the same house.

That's our hope for you. Shannon and I hope that you will use the tools in this book to beautifully transform your relationships and build the home life you've always dreamed of. As a recap, the new tools we've recommended for your home improvement toolbox are . . .

Kindness rather than selfishness,

Gratitude rather than disrespect,

Love rather than apathy,

Compromise rather than conflict,

Forgiveness rather than resentment,

Communication rather than confusion,

Trust rather than control,

Compassion rather than hurtfulness,

Patience rather than anger,

Organization rather than disorganization,

Fun rather than boredom,

and *Connection* rather than distraction.

Beyond recommending these home improvement tools, I've invited you to draw up your plans for change and to initiate change at home by using these tools yourself (to DIY) before expecting your family to use them. Initiative and creativity will help your family go all-in with needed home improvements. I've also encouraged you to put in the necessary sweat equity that home improvement requires. With this type of time and effort, your hard work will surely pay off in the form of amazing big reveal moments.

I do want to recommend one more important home improvement tool—home maintenance. You already know how much work housecleaning can be. Interestingly, cleaning a house can take hours; messing it up again can take seconds. That's why cleaning a little every day makes sense. Few of us have chunks of time to clean, but we all have a few minutes here and there to pick up and clean up after ourselves.

Home life is similar. Developing loving, supportive relationships with our spouse and children takes a long time; it's something that can't be done in a few seconds but can be undone in a few seconds. For this reason, I recommend that couples and families invest in daily "home maintenance."

In terms of home life, home maintenance simply means using all the home improvement tools listed above on an ongoing basis. Rather than waiting until major relationship "messes" pop up or major relationship "repairs" are needed, use your home improvement tools to prevent or minimize messes and repairs. Or if a major mess sneaks up on you, recognize it and respond with cleanup and repair efforts as quickly as possible. Responsiveness like this can help you sustain your home improvement efforts rather than continually having to make major home improvements.

And, of course, big-ticket home improvement can be costly. So people dreaming of a new kitchen or modernized bathroom might put it off because they think they can't afford it. Or they may say, "We'll just get a newer house." However, beautiful home improvements are possible with the right professional guidance and careful budgeting.

Similarly, people sometimes think, "Our marriage and

family life will never get any better. Maybe we'd be better off with someone else." People can't abandon their marriages and families as easily as they can houses. Many people give up and distance themselves emotionally from their loved ones. In some cases, they even turn their backs and walk away. These are sad moves with far-reaching consequences for the person who leaves and the people who are left behind.

As with literal home improvement, couples are wiser to invest in their current marriage and family life than to falsely believe that the grass will be greener in someone else's yard. Shannon and I have experienced this truth over and over again in our years of marriage and family counseling. That's one of the main reasons we take great joy in sharing with you *The DIY Guide to Building a Family That Lasts*. We truly believe the ideas we've shared here can encourage you and change the way you and your loved ones see and treat each other. We believe you can totally "afford" these home improvements!

We also believe you're totally capable of sustaining an amazing home life. You'll need daily home maintenance, which is doing over and over again the essentials of home improvement. But you'll also need another kind of "do-over." You and your loved ones will sometimes fall short in your home improvement efforts. You can and should allow each other do-overs to right your wrongs. For example, if you speak harshly to your spouse or children, you can ask for a do-over. "I'm so sorry. Let me try that again." Or if your children treat you or each other in an unkind or disrespectful way, you can coach them by saying, "How you handled that is not okay with me. Try handling it this way . . . " Thank them for their improved do-over, and move on. Shannon and I call this "the art of the do-over." With practice, couples and families can use this amazing relationship skill to assist them with daily home maintenance and with sustaining their all-in home improvement efforts.

From kindness (chapter 1) to home maintenance and all in between, Shannon and I thoroughly enjoyed developing the many parallels in literal home improvement and relational home improvement. These are ideas that we regularly use in our counseling. We hope you've enjoyed the book as much as we enjoyed writing it. And we wish you and your loved ones well as you work on home improvement together!

HOME LIFE INSPECTION QUIZ

HOME INSPECTIONS are required when building a home or doing major home renovations. Inspectors must ensure a home is safe and ready for occupancy. Similarly, families should regularly inspect their home life to ensure that their relationships are satisfying. Home life inspections can also help families identify which areas of home life may need improvement. To aid families with their home life inspections, Shannon and I created the Home Life Inspection Quiz.

Completing the Home Life Inspection Quiz will help you identify which of twelve areas in your home life may be due for renovation. Within each of the twelve areas listed below, you'll see two questions. The first question will get you thinking about your readiness to lead your family in the various areas of home life. When answering these questions, you may want to ask yourself, "What would my family say is true about me?" The second question in each of the twelve sets of questions is about you and your family as a whole. When answering these questions, consider interactions between everyone living in your home and ask yourself, "How are we doing as a group?"

The answer options for each question are "satisfied" and "needs improvement." Choosing satisfied means you're typically satisfied in that area of home life even if it's not perfect. Choosing "needs improvement" means you believe you and/or your family need improvement in that area of home life.

Try not to overthink the wording of the questions but instead, answer based on your interpretation of the questions. Your answers will result in a satisfaction rating as well as help guide you in planning your family's home life renovations.

. . . .

For each question below, select either "satisfied" or "needs improvement."

KINDNESS

As an individual, I typically share my time, space, and possessions with my family.

Satisfied _____   **Needs improvement** _____

As a family, we typically share our time, space, and possessions with each other.

Satisfied _____   **Needs improvement** _____

GRATITUDE

As an individual, I typically respect my family through my attitudes, words, and behaviors.

Satisfied _____   **Needs improvement** _____

As a family, we typically respect each other through our attitudes, words, and behaviors.

Satisfied _____   **Needs improvement** _____

LOVE

As an individual, I am typically attentive to and appreciative of my family.

Satisfied _____   **Needs improvement** _____

As a family, we are typically attentive to and appreciative of each other.

Satisfied _____   **Needs improvement** _____

COMPROMISE

As an individual, I am typically able to handle conflict with my family calmly and fairly.

Satisfied _____   **Needs improvement** _____

As a family, we are typically able to handle conflict with each other calmly and fairly.

Satisfied _____   **Needs improvement** _____

FORGIVENESS

As an individual, I typically am not resentful and do not hold grudges against my family.

Satisfied _____   **Needs improvement** _____

As a family, we typically are not resentful and do not hold grudges against each other.

Satisfied _____   **Needs improvement** _____

COMMUNICATION

As an individual, I typically express my thoughts and feelings in ways that encourage my family.

Satisfied _____   **Needs improvement** _____

As a family, we typically express our thoughts and feelings in ways that encourage each other.

Satisfied _____   **Needs improvement** _____

TRUST

As an individual, I typically do not attempt to control my family.

Satisfied _____   **Needs improvement** _____

As a family, we typically do not attempt to control each other.

Satisfied _____   **Needs improvement** _____

COMPASSION

As an individual, I typically recognize when a family member is struggling and respond in sensitive, supportive ways.

Satisfied _____   **Needs improvement** _____

As a family, we typically recognize when one of us is struggling and respond in sensitive, supportive ways.

Satisfied _____   **Needs improvement** _____

PATIENCE

As an individual, I typically manage my anger toward my family in positive ways.

Satisfied _____   **Needs improvement** _____

As a family, we typically manage our anger toward each other in positive ways.

Satisfied _____   **Needs improvement** _____

ORGANIZATION

As an individual, I am typically flexible and not easily stressed out by shifts in my family's schedule.

Satisfied _____   **Needs improvement** _____

As a family, we are typically flexible and not easily stressed out by shifts in our schedule.

Satisfied _____   **Needs improvement** _____

FUN

As an individual, I typically make time to rest and recharge in creative ways with my family.

Satisfied _____   **Needs improvement** _____

As a family, we typically make time to rest and recharge in creative ways with each other.

Satisfied _____   **Needs improvement** _____

CONNECTION

As an individual, I typically engage with my family rather than allowing less important things to distract me.

Satisfied _____   **Needs improvement** _____

As a family, we typically engage with each other rather than allowing less important things to distract us.

Satisfied _____   **Needs improvement** _____

BONUS QUESTION

Overall, my family and I typically work as a team to make needed home life improvements.

Satisfied _____   **Needs improvement** _____

. . . .

Your score

Including the bonus question, there are 25 possible "satisfied" answers. For each "satisfied" you selected, give yourself 4 points. For example, if you selected "satisfied" 10 times, that would equal 40 points; or, if you selected "satisfied" 20 times, that would equal 80 points. Next, think of your total points as a percentage and that percentage as your percentage of home life satisfaction. Thus, the person with 40 points has a 40% home life satisfaction; the person with

80 points has an 80% home life satisfaction. (Note: It's important to remember that the Home Life Inspection Quiz is a non-scientific quiz, is based only on your answers for these 12 areas of home life, and is not a comprehensive measure of home life satisfaction.)

How many times did you answer "satisfied"?

_____ x 4 = _____%

With your home life satisfaction rating in mind, review the areas of home life with which you are satisfied. Talk with your family and celebrate the success you and they have accomplished in these areas. Discuss how it is you and they can sustain ongoing success in these areas.

For areas of home life you rated as "needs improvement," think about changes you and your family need to make. Talk with them about how you and they can work together to implement needed changes. For inspiration and ideas, read and implement the many helpful tools found in *The DIY Guide to Building a Family That Lasts.*

The Home Life Inspection Quiz can help you right now by generating thought and discussion with your family about where you and they are succeeding and where home life improvement may be needed. Beyond helping guide you in currently needed improvements, use the Home Life Inspection Quiz again and again for periodic home life maintenance.

ACKNOWLEDGMENTS

SPECIAL THANKS to all the couples who have shared with us their home life improvement journeys. We are also indebted to our own families with whom we have shared the family journey.

Thanks also to Anita Hall, Dr. Chapman's administrative assistant. And, of course, this book would not have become a reality without the Northfield Publishing team: John Hinkley, Betsey Newenhuyse, Zack Williamson, Janis Todd, and so many more.

NOTES

Chapter Two: INCREASING GRATITUDE

1. Proverbs 15:1.

Chapter Three: CULTIVATING LOVE

1. 1 Corinthians 13:4–8.

Chapter Five: CHOOSING FORGIVENESS

1. Corrie ten Boom, *Clippings from My Notebook* (Thorndike, ME: Thorndike Press, 1982), 23.

2. https://www.goodreads.com/quotes/895079-a-happy-marriage-is-the-union-of-two-good-forgivers. In *A Quiet Knowing*, it says: "The late Robert Quinlan once described marriage as 'the union of two good forgivers'" (Gigi Graham Tchividjian with Ruth Bell Graham, *A Quiet Knowing: Devotional Thoughts for Troubled Times* [Nashville: W Publishing Group, 2001], 90).

3. Gary Chapman and Jennifer Thomas, *When Sorry Isn't Enough* (Chicago: Northfield, 2013).

Chapter Six: IMPROVING COMMUNICATION

1. "They May Forget What You Said, but They Will Never Forget How You Made Them Feel," Quote Investigator, https://quoteinvestigator.com/2014/04/06/they-feel/.

Chapter Seven: ENHANCING TRUST

1. Erik Erikson, *Identity and the Life Cycle* (New York: International Universities Press, 1959).

2. Rudolf Dreikurs and Vicki Stoltz, *Children: The Challenge* (New York: Hawthorn/Dutton, 1964).

3. Haim G. Ginott, *Between Parent and Child: Revised and Updated: The Bestselling Classic That Revolutionized Parent-Child Communication*, revised and expanded by Alice Ginott and H. Wallace Goddard (New York: Three Rivers Press, 2003).

4. Lenore Skenazy, *Free-Range Kids, How to Raise Safe, Self-Reliant Children (Without Going Nuts With Worry)* (San Francisco: Jossey-Bass, 2009).

5. Ben Schott, "Velcro Parents," *New York Times*, August 30, 2010, https://schott.blogs.nytimes.com/2010/08/30/velcro-parents/.

6. Amy Chua, *Battle Hymn of the Tiger Mother* (New York: Penguin Press, 2011).

7. Dallas Willard, *Life Without Lack: Living in the Fullness of Psalm 23* (Nashville: Thomas Nelson, 2018), 199.

Chapter Eight: DEVELOPING COMPASSION

1. The Center for Compassion and Altruism Research and Education, Stanford University, ccare.stanford.edu; CCARE at Stanford University, "Power of Compassion & Importance of the Work of CCARE," YouTube video, April 22, 2015, https://www.youtube.com/watch?v=rUi40yTXrjY.

2. Brian Morton, "Falser Words Were Never Spoken," *New York Times*, August 29, 2011, https://www.nytimes.com/2011/08/30/opinion/falser-words-were-never-spoken.html.

3. The Center for Compassion and Altruism Research and Education, Stanford University, ccare.stanford.edu;

CCARE at Stanford University, "Power of Compassion & Importance of the Work of CCARE," YouTube video, April 22, 2015, https://www.youtube.com/watch?v=rUi40yTXrjY.

Chapter Nine: INCREASING PATIENCE

1. Proverbs 29:11.

Chapter Ten: GETTING ORGANIZED

1. George Doran, "There's a S.M.A.R.T. Way to Write Management's Goals and Objectives," *Management Review* 70, no. 11 (1981): 35–36, https://community.mis.temple.edu/mis0855002fall2015/files/2015/10/S.M.A.R.T-Way-Management-Review.pdf.

2. James Prochaska and Carlo DiClemente, "Transtheoretical Therapy: Toward a More Integrative Model of Change," *Psychotherapy Theory Research & Practice* 19, no. 3 (1982): 276–88.

Chapter Eleven: CREATING FUN

1. C. S. Lewis, *Surprised by Joy: The Shape of My Early Life* (San Diego: Harcourt Brace, 1955), 23.

Chapter Twelve: BUILDING CONNECTION

1. Common Sense Media, https://www.commonsensemedia.org/device-free-dinner.

2. Gary Chapman and Ramon Presson, *101 Conversation Starters for Couples* (Chicago: Northfield, 2012).

3. Gary Chapman and Ramon Presson, *101 Conversation Starters for Families* (Chicago: Northfield, 2012).

4. Gary Chapman and Clarence Shuler, *Choose Greatness: 11 Wise Decisions That Brave Young Men Make* (Chicago: Northfield, 2019).

ABOUT THE AUTHORS

DR. GARY CHAPMAN has a passion for helping people form lasting relationships. He is the bestselling author of The 5 Love Languages® series and director of Marriage and Family Life Consultants, Inc. Gary travels the world presenting seminars, and his radio programs air on more than 400 stations. For more information, visit www.5lovelanguages.com.

DR. SHANNON WARDEN is an author, speaker, counselor, and teacher committed to helping people build healthy relationships. She is a faculty member in the Department of Counseling at Wake Forest University in Winston-Salem, NC, and she is the director of counseling and women's ministries at nearby Triad Baptist Church. She and her husband, Stephen, have been married for more than twenty years and have three children (Avery, Carson, and Presley). For the latest on Shannon's life and work, check out her website at www.shannonwarden.com

WHAT SEPARATES HAPPY MARRIAGES FROM MISERABLE ONES?

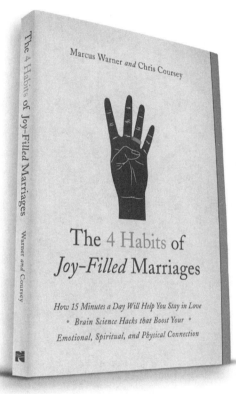

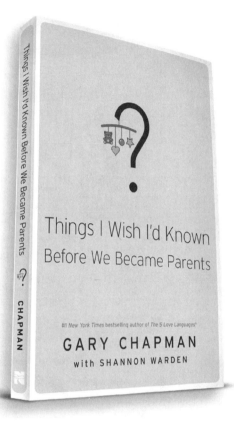

IF GOD IS LOVE, WHY DOESN'T EVERYONE *FEEL* LOVED BY HIM?

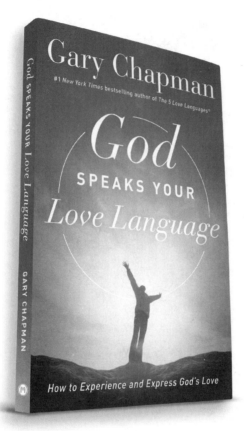

HOW TO RAISE A GODLY MAN, NOT A FULL-GROWN BOY.

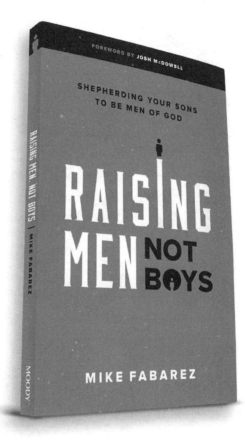

Raising Men, Not Boys is about navigating the times and raising a generation of men on godly principles—sons who are ready, able, and motivated to represent God during their days of sojourn on this earth. Parents will be equipped to set the spiritual trajectory of sons so that they launch into godly manhood, rather than flounder in prolonged immaturity.

978-0-8024-1657-5 | also available as an eBook